Encyclopedia of Acting Techniques

Encyclopedia of Acting Techniques

Illustrated instruction, examples and advice for
improving acting techniques and stage presence –
from tragedy to comedy, epic to farce

John Perry

BETTERWAY BOOKS

TO STAN

A QUARTO BOOK
© 1997 Quarto Inc.

First published in North America in
1997 by Betterway Books,
an imprint of F&W Publications,
1507 Dana Avenue,
Cincinnati, OH 45207

Designed and produced by
Quarto Publishing plc,
The Old Brewery,
6 Blundell Street,
London N7 9BH

ISBN 1-55870-456-6

Senior editor Sally MacEachern
Editor Miranda Stonor
Art editors Clare Baggaley,
Julie Francis
Designer Tanya Devonshire-Jones
Illustrators Ian Mitchell, Coral Mula
Photographer Paul Forrester
Picture researcher Angela
Anderson
Picture research manager Giulia
Hetherington
Assistant art director Penny Cobb
Art director Moira Clinch

Typeset by Type Technique,
London W1
Manufactured in Malaysia by
C. H. Colour Scan Sdn. Bhd.
Printed in Singapore by Star
Standard Industries (Pte) Ltd.

Contents

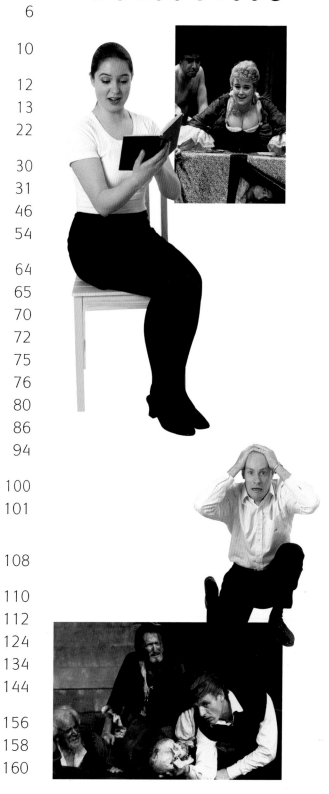

Introduction

Aspects of Acting

Theatre has always developed as a communal, sometimes sacred activity. In our modern technological society, it still remains a cooperative social art. A group of artists – writers, actors, designers, painters and sculptors – as well as engineers, administrators and producers create a piece of theatre that is ultimately to be observed by another group, which is the group of strangers called the audience.

Acting is is about communication – not only between actor and audience but also between actors throughout the entire rehearsal process. Everyone is obliged to articulate and communicate their ideas. In modern theatre, the relationship between the actor and the director is a constant and intimate act of communication. Indeed, the whole life of the actor is a continuous job of communication.

Unlike the painter or the sculptor, the actor has no canvas or object to look at when his or her work is finished. As an actor, you are your own material. When others assess your work, they will talk about you: your body, your voice, your feelings and your imagination. While this may feel intrusive and exposing, it is precisely this which makes your work unique. If you bring your own experience to a role, you avoid resorting to clichés and you make possible an interpretation that has originality and humanity, and is distinctly yours.

The Craft of Acting

The craft of the actor is to reveal the way human beings live in the world. The actor can show us ordinary behavior in a new light or at a different angle. By revealing character, or exposing a dramatic situation, the actor is also exposed, because the actor can only make these things seem real and human by connecting them with his or her own imagination and experience.

Revelation is the entire object of the actor's craft. Different actors reveal themselves in different ways. Some require the physical trappings of transformation; beards and false noses, etc. Some use physical cues or "hooks" to transform themselves, and some use psychological cues. There is no difference between these, so long as they are working to create the truth of the play and the character they are portraying.

Truthfulness in acting means being truthful to the humanity of the character within the world that is enacted in the play. For example, classical tragedy, farce, contemporary domestic drama and musicals present wildly different worlds, and truthful acting will be different for each.

The actor who cannot act truthfully is unconvincing. The untruthful actor either cannot observe truthfully, or cannot convey that truth clearly within the artificial convention of the world of the play. You can only show a character truthfully through compassionate observation. This is not the same as sympathy. You need not like, respect or even understand the character you are becoming, but you must be prepared to connect with him or her on a human level, and to see the world from his or her angle. This is your best chance to play others without judgement, either good or bad. Judgement is the prerogative of the audience, not the actor.

Actors should compassionately observe themselves. Since you are your own material, you will have to understand yourself quite thoroughly if you are to use yourself fully in the craft. You cannot do this if you shade your observations with flattery or self-hatred. Both of these are self-indulgences that you should try to avoid!

Like all crafts, the craft of acting is specific. Bertolt Brecht, the German playwright, poet and director, talked admiringly of actors who agonize over the choice of small personal props. It is not just in physical choices that specificity is required – in all decisions of character and action the good actor works untiringly for the exactly correct choice.

Acting Games and Exercises

This book describes comprehensively the playful, game-based aspects of acting. All of the exercises given here are best worked in a group or with a partner. That way you can explore the ideas by making them physical through the exercises. Physically working at an idea or a problem is central to the craft of the actor. The actor always wants to be "doing" or "being" or "transforming."

I hope that in going through this book, you will discover, or be reminded of, the demands that acting makes upon the actor, as well as the many pleasures it offers. Becoming an actor is a process that may last for your whole life. However far you travel, I hope you do so with pleasure, and that this book becomes part of the journey.

Note: The word "actor" is used throughout the book to refer to both male and female players.

Equipment

The equipment required for acting is relatively simple, consisting mainly of useful clothing, and some items for taking notes and for vocal practice.

How to Dress

Do not hide behind your clothes or indulge in "personality dressing" with clothes that are strong on image and weak on practicality. While it is useful to dress neatly to audition, rehearsal clothes should be loose, comfortable and easy to move in. Do not arrive in tight dresses or high heels. This restricts what can be done in rehearsal and will irritate the other players.

A sense of humor and a playful attitude will help you through early rehearsals.

Dressing for Movement

It is very important that you are warm at the beginning of a movement class. You should always stretch and warm up your muscles before you start, but clothing also helps. You should start the session in a tracksuit, or a tracksuit bottom and a T-shirt. Wear an all-in-one leotard underneath. Pay special attention to your feet; make sure they are warm and look after them. Thick socks can sometimes be used by themselves if the floor is suitable. Bare feet are sometimes appropriate, depending on the movement you are doing. Good contact with the floor helps you to feel "grounded" and strong. Jazz shoes have a very

character shoes

jazz shoes

Dressing for Style

When rehearsing classical work or when playing characters of a certain class, you should have one or two items of costume that make you feel different early in rehearsal. Women should have a motley skirt, which is a full-length skirt, held at the waist and hanging from the hips. It is easily made from a semicircle of medium-weight natural fabric. Character shoes, which are leather shoes with a block heel, help to give some physical elevation and projection.

Men should have a well-fitting pair of black oxford shoes, black formal pants and two white shirts, one with a collar and one without as well as a starched wing collar with studs, cufflinks and a cummerbund, which is a broad strip of material wrapped around the waist. The object is not to aquire a complete wardrobe, but to have enough of the elements of costume to give you the sensation of formal dress early in rehearsal.

thin sole, so you can also feel the floor when wearing them. They are useful if you are doing quick, turning work as they absorb the friction of the floor and so protect you.

The Leotard

The actors who illustrate the exercises in this book are usually wearing a leotard. This is an important piece of clothing because it allows you to work as if you are naked and untrammeled by clothes, which always impose a certain style on your work. The leotard is useful for physical transformation, because it requires all the work to be done by your body, unaided by the weight, volume or style of your clothes. Some very specific movement work requires a leotard, and sometimes you might enjoy the freedom to move around in one.

Buy a leotard in which you can work comfortably – there are a number of different styles. Get used to the shape of your body, and if you can't learn to love it, learn to put up with it – it will improve with use! You may feel self-conscious initially, but this will pass. Remember that actors are usually far too self-obsessed to pay the slightest attention to you!

Bits and Pieces

You should have a pencil, a notebook and a diary in order to record all the sensations, ideas and observations that you may wish to remember and use in your work. You will learn with practice what may be of use to you and should work to develop a professional style of taking notes.

A dictating machine or cassette player is useful for vocal practice, practicing accents, recording notes and playing music to yourself that is appropriate to the mood of the work you are about to do.

The leotard is useful for the movement class and for physical "transformation."

Acting
Techniques

Chapter 1

The Actor's Frame of Mind

Individual Preparation

This section deals with the way you prepare yourself for acting work. Preparation is a skill that requires practice. It may take effort at first but, once the habit is established, a few minutes a day as a physical reminder may be all that is required.

First, you should focus on your physical and mental state. Let the floor take your weight while you release tension; concentrate, but remain in a relaxed state both physically and mentally. Don't be alarmed at instructions to talk to your body – they work! If you try to push and pull your body into shape, you will only reinforce bad habits. Once your body gets used to being talked to, it will do as it's told! Also remember that *relaxed* doesn't mean *collapsed*. The object is to start work in a physical and mental state that is alert and receptive to whatever the rehearsal might give or demand.

The work takes a significant amount of time, and you will have to program it into your day. This is easy when you are "between jobs." It is essential to practice your individual preparation on these occasions, but you should also remember that it is just as important when you are under pressure and you think you can't possibly spare the time. You may only lie down for 10 minutes, but you must do it, and your preparation will probably save you time in the long run.

To obtain the right frame of mind as an actor you should first relax physically and mentally.

Relaxation

Allow two periods a week for this when you can be undisturbed. Find somewhere cozy and warm. Do this exercise on a rug if you wish, and play some soothing music. If you fall asleep, don't worry.

You should put aside 20 minutes for the whole exercise.

Exercise

How to Relax

1 Sit on the floor with your legs extended. Draw up your knees and wrap your arms around them so you are balancing on your coccyx (tailbone). Close your eyes and let your breathing be easy. Don't hold your breath.

2 Keeping your eyes closed and your breathing easy, extend your legs and arms. Enjoy balancing. Feel easy. Do not strain yourself!

3 Gently ease yourself down to the floor so that you are lying on your back. Lift your legs to about 30 degrees from the floor. Hold the position for a count of 10, and lower. Repeat if you wish, but

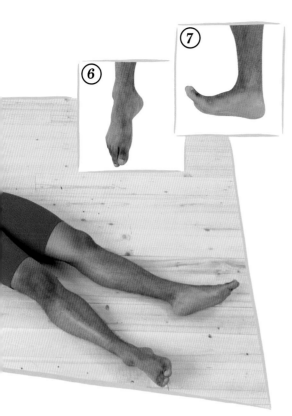

Tape Talk-through

Let your breathing be light and easy. Make yourself comfortable on the floor, because you will be there for some time. Rest for 20 seconds. Don't fidget, or try to do anything; let your imagination do the work. Your ankles, wrists, elbows and knees are free to move, but they do not. Imagine that the tips of your fingers and the tips of your toes are hollow, like tubes. Sense the tips of your fingers and toes. Rest for 20 seconds. Imagine that a heavy substance is being poured into the tips of the fingers of your right hand; now your left hand . . . . Your wrists feel very heavy . . . your elbows . . . now your shoulders. Everything is very heavy. Rest for 20 seconds.

Your breathing is light and easy. Imagine weight is pouring through the toes of your right leg; now your left leg. Your ankles are heavy . . . so are your knees . . . and your pelvis. Your legs and arms are very heavy. Let them rest for 20 seconds.

Your breathing is light and easy. Let weight flood into your torso so that only your head remains light. Let the weight from your shoulders flood into your head. Let your head roll to the side if it is too heavy. Your whole body is massively heavy. Let it rest for 20 seconds. Imagine that the floor is bearing on your heavy body, as though your body is held in a huge hand. Rest for 60 seconds.

Let the weight flood away through the fingers of your right hand . . . and your left hand . . . and your right leg . . . and your left leg . . . . Let it flood from your body through your limbs and away. You feel incredibly light. Your body only just seems to brush the floor. Rest for 60 seconds.

Allow your body to return to its normal feeling of your own weight: your arms . . . shoulders . . . legs . . . pelvis . . . torso . . . neck and head . . . . Flex and stretch your fingers . . . your arms . . . your legs . . . . Wake up!

don't over-exert yourself. Lower your legs and let the stomach muscles relax. Enjoy the sensation.

4 Clench your left fist, so you can feel the tension in your arm.

5 Relax and enjoy the sensation. Repeat with the right arm. Relax.

6 Point the right foot gently, and feel the tension in your leg muscles. Relax.

7 Flex your right foot, and feel the slight tension in your leg. Relax. Repeat with the left foot. Relax. Enjoy the sensation.

You are now going to relax your body on to the floor. When you have followed this through a couple of times, you could speak it on to a tape and play it to yourself.

Focus and Concentration

Use a warm room without drafts. This is a
focusing exercise, and is directed at
muscular release.

You can use this exercise as a substitute for the relaxation exercise on pages 14-15.

Muscular Focus

1 Lie down on your back and rest your head on a book about 2in (5cm) thick. Draw up your feet so that your knees point to the ceiling. Let your eyes rest easily (do not stare) on a point on the ceiling. Do not close your eyes.

2 Concentrate on the *out*-breath. Let the *in*-breath take care of itself.

3 Imagine your face is "radiating" into the space.

4 Imagine the top of your head is tending towards the wall behind it.

5 Without doing anything, say to yourself: "My neck is free, my spine is lengthening and my back is widening." The small of your back would like to rest on the floor. Let it, but do not force it.

6 Imagine your knees are suspended from the ceiling on strings. Let your hip joints be free.

7 Talk yourself through this muscular focus for no less than 15 minutes. If you feel a tension, don't fidget but focus your mind on it. You will find that it will release itself. If you feel any muscular pain, *stop*.

Salutation to the Sun

This easily learned cycle of stretch-and-breathe exercises will take about three minutes to complete once the positions have been learned. Although this is a yoga exercise, it is more dynamic than is usual in yoga. The cycle should be worked with light, quick energy, staying with the positions for no more than a few seconds. Synchronizing movement and breathing, the cycle ventilates the lungs, oxygenates and steps up the flow of blood through the body, and tones the nervous system by flexing the spinal column. ◗

This exercise is much easier in practice than it may sound!

Exercise

Stretching and Breathing

1 *Exhale* fully.

2 Link your thumbs and swing back, arching the spine. *Inhale*.

3 Push your head toward your knees. Your hands should be level with your ankles. *Exhale*.

4 Put your head back; your spine should be slightly arched. One leg should be extended backward with the other leg bent in front. *Inhale*.

5 Put your feet flat on the ground. Look toward your knees. *Hold your breath*.

6 Your toes should be arched to the floor. Your spine should be arched. Don't lie flat! *Exhale*.

7 Push upwards from 6. Arch your

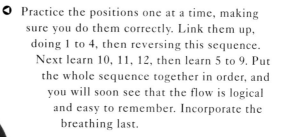

● Practice the positions one at a time, making sure you do them correctly. Link them up, doing 1 to 4, then reversing this sequence. Next learn 10, 11, 12, then learn 5 to 9. Put the whole sequence together in order, and you will soon see that the flow is logical and easy to remember. Incorporate the breathing last.

spine the other way. *Inhale.*

8 Repeat step 5. Put your feet on the ground. Look toward your knees. *Hold your breath.*

9 Repeat step 4. Put your head back; your spine should be slightly arched. One leg should be extended backward with the other leg bent in front. *Hold your breath.*

10 Repeat step 3. Push your head toward your knees. Your hands should be level with your ankles. *Exhale.*

11 Repeat step 2. Link your thumbs and swing back, arching the spine. *Inhale.*

12 Repeat step 1. *Exhale.*

Imaginative Warm-ups

When you "endow" an object or a person in an imaginative warm-up, you imagine that they have certain specific qualities and you behave towards them as though they actually possessed those qualities. Endowment requires *belief*. An actor can treat a fellow actor as though she were his mother, knowing she is not his mother. He can treat an object as a fluttering bird. It is the belief of the audience in the actions of the actor that creates theatrical truth.

Endowments make specific use of your imagination and the exercises that follow are imaginative warm-ups, starting with a simple one and becoming more complicated. You will no doubt find many occasions to use them in the course of your rehearsal preparation.

Endowing a Chair as a Throne

1 The actress sees the chair as her beautifully upholstered and embellished throne. She feels superior to the space around it; she becomes the Queen.
2 She regards the wall and sees a sea of people. They are cheering, and she deigns to respond. She glides to the throne, and graciously sits.
3 She plays this scenario through again, endowing a flashlight as a scepter and a sugar bowl as an orb, with a baking dish as a crown.

Endowing a Chair as a Vicious Dog

1 The actor behaves towards the chair as though it is a vicious dog. He tries to get past the dog by calming it, and is very wary of it. As the actor plays with the endowment, he discovers *who*, *where* and *what* he is doing.

2 The actor plays again. He is a burglar in a mansion. Escaping with the goods, he comes face to face with a vicious dog.

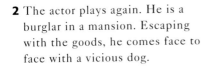

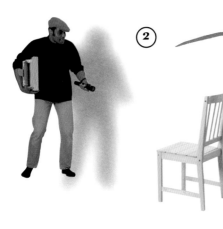

3 The actor can continue to develop this scenario. He can develop the story, but that isn't his skill – an actor is not a writer, so he'll probably embellish the circumstances, his character or his relationship with the dog (the chair). Will he make friends with it or silence it?

Exercise

Endowing a Glass of Water

---

1 The actor enters the room and sees the glass.
2 He wants to drink the liquid but suspects it.
3 He tests the liquid.
4 Finally, on impulse, he swallows it.
5 It is lethal poison . . . .

The actor repeats the exercise, playing each moment and clarifying the improvisation *beat* by *beat*. He plays a series of impulses. He is a man returning to the house of his estranged wife. She has left refreshment for him, as in happier days. The first impulse is that he enters expecting to greet his wife – but she isn't there.

His second impulse is that he sees the glass. He smiles, recognizing the social gesture of leaving the drink for him. His third impulse is that he takes the glass to drink.

His fourth impulse is that he has another thought. The glass looks different.

At the fifth impulse, he becomes suspicious. He thinks she's trying to poison him. With his sixth impulse he becomes obsessed with testing the liquid. The seventh impulse: he laughs at his suspicions. He drinks it in one gulp.

Group Work

Group exercises and group play are useful throughout the rehearsal process. Although they do not directly contribute to text or character analysis, they do contribute to the atmosphere in which this work will be done.

Group play has specific uses because it makes everybody focus on the group. Individuals can find moments to say things to each other which would be more difficult during the "serious" periods of script rehearsal. Group work can also remind everyone of the importance of their role, however small their part, and can allow everyone to focus on the fact that the group, and ultimately the production, is bigger than the sum of its parts.

Group dynamics are often forgotten in the rehearsal process. Group work will sometimes happen at the start of rehearsals and then get forgotten once work on the script begins. The company then fragments, only meeting in twos and threes to rehearse with the director. The company then has to put itself together again, late in the rehearsal process. If it does not do this, early performances may be wooden and unconvincing because the company is getting used to working together once more.

The Rehearsal Room

Everyone who has any experience of rehearsal knows the difference between an atmosphere that is relaxed, creative and disciplined, and one that is tense, full of unspoken negativity and can be "cut with a knife." If you want to get the best from rehearsals, you must work for the following atmospheres in the rehearsal room.

A Safe Atmosphere

Every member of the cast must feel that they can try out anything in rehearsal without being laughed at or humiliated if it goes wrong. This means that, though you can have a laugh in rehearsal, you must always have total respect for work taking place on the rehearsal floor. To laugh at someone while they are working is the most destructive thing you can do.

• •

The exercise illustrated here is for three players, but the variations are endless. It can be done with five or more players standing in a circle.

This well-known exercise promotes focus, physical trust and sensitive group work. The atmosphere among the players must be calm and alert. The idea is that one person gives the group total physical trust. The rest of the group facilitates this. It must never be done as a gymnastic exercise or as "dares," because any group feeling will then be destroyed.

Exercise

Trust Falling

1 Find a space where you are not cramped, and can increase the space you use if you wish. One person stands in the middle. He or she closes their eyes. The others place their hands on the person and rock them. The person being moved places his feet together, releases the ankles, wrists and neck, but holds on slightly behind the knees and in the small of the back (otherwise he or she becomes a "dead-weight"). The person in the middle closes his eyes and lets his chin drop to his chest.

2 The rest of the group move the person in the middle, moving him or her gently between each other. It is possible to increase the distance the person moves and to vary the rhythm of movement, but the group must be sensitive to any tension in the person being moved, and decrease the action if the person shows muscular tension or if they laugh from nerves, for example.

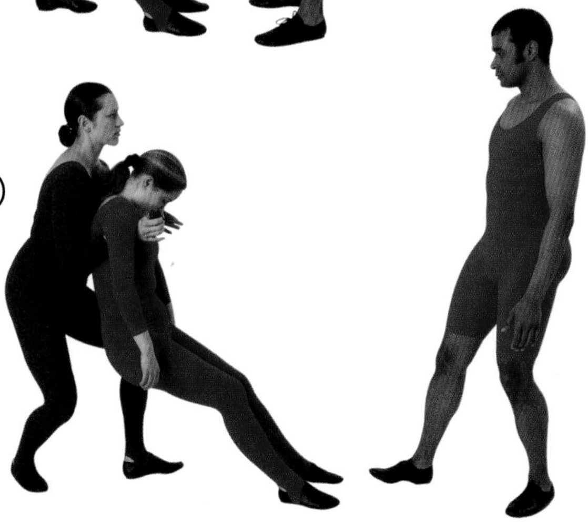

3 Don't feel you have to *do* all the time. You can hold the person still, or play very gently with the point of balance. Start and finish with hands on the person in the middle.

An Atmosphere of Trust

Whatever the style of the play, it is useful to be physically easy with your fellow players. Physical awkwardness or embarrassment will limit the choices you can make while developing your role and relationship. Also, you need a certain amount of personal trust, so you can make suggestions if a scene is blocked and feel free to ask for something different from your acting partner.

Saying yes is harder than it sounds. In ordinary life, most of us automatically say "no," so "say-yes-and-do-it" games can be scary at first . Once you've broken the "hang-on-a-minute-while-I-think-of-something" barrier, a lot of exuberant energy is released, and a lot of relieved hilarity!

Warm up with simple instruction and copying games. This joining-in exercise is an example.

Exercise

Joining In

1 The group walks freely, filling the whole available floor space. Walk towards the gaps as they appear in the pattern you make. See each other with "live eyes" – don't glaze your eyes or stare at each other.

2 Any individual can begin with a simple instruction, such as "opening." Everyone stops and does this.

3 Everybody then walks as before.

4 The same person or another leader says "squatting." Everybody then squats.

5 Walk as before.

6 Another instruction is given, such as "sitting," and everybody sits.

A simple game like this can be extended by using a movement style such as floating or molding (see the Earth, Water, Air and Fire exercise on pages 42–3), or developed by copying or imitating the leader. Leadership can be passed round freely by touch-tagging. Avoid games in which people are "out." Keep the group together!

For the exercise below you should work in pairs. The first person starts an action (a physical mime, such as skiing, brushing teeth or playing tennis). The partner asks, "What are you doing?" The first person lies. The second person has to act out the lie.

The first person asks, "What are you doing?" The partner lies, and then the first person must act out the lie. And so on.

Now try with a group of four, using this structure to build up and change improvisations. One person begins a physical action, such as swimming. Another person "swims" out to him, they improvise, another actor swims in like a shark, and so on, building up the improvisation.

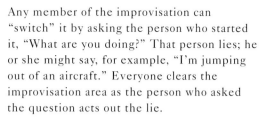

This play improvisation will help to make a lively, creative atmosphere in the rehearsal room.

Exercise

I'm Lying

1 Start the game in pairs. Chloe asks, "What are you doing?" Tim lies: "I'm jumping up and down."
2 Chloe jumps up and down. Tim then asks, "What are you doing?" Chloe lies: "I'm falling from a great height."
3 Tim pretends to do this.

This game can also be played in a group. One person starts to mime an action. The group builds up the improvisation by joining in.

Any member of the improvisation can "switch" it by asking the person who started it, "What are you doing?" That person lies; he or she might say, for example, "I'm jumping out of an aircraft." Everyone clears the improvisation area as the person who asked the question acts out the lie.

Others join in and build on the scenarios as before. These are "play" improvisations, designed to create lively, spontaneous energy, and to "break the ice" in a group of people beginning to work towards a play. Such improvisations rarely produce usable material, but they are important in establishing the atmosphere of the rehearsal room.

Sometimes the whole group will be in the improvisation, which can be *changed* at any time by any member of the group asking the person who started the action, "What are you doing?"

The person who started the improvisation *lies*. The person who asked the question mimes the lie. The others join in, and so on.

A Demanding Atmosphere

Each individual should feel challenged by the group. If the rehearsal atmosphere is safe, then everybody's performance is enhanced, and individuals surpass themselves. There needs to be a group culture of hard work, during and between rehearsals, and energy for the whole production rather than just for your own part. Weaker members of the group will conform to this culture if the stronger members take responsibility and set the pace. The opposite is possible in a bad group, where the weakest pull the others down, individuals collude with each other not to confront shoddy work, and it becomes dangerous to do any work for fear of being ridiculed. Here are some exercises aimed at group focus and concentration.

The well-known game below is useful as a concentration warm-up.

Exercise

Mirrors in Pairs and Groups

1 Stand opposite your partner. One person, the "leader," begins to move and his or her partner, the "follower," mirrors them by copying the action.

2 The idea is to create a "mirror" impression, with both partners moving exactly together.

3 Copy everything, including facial expressions and all details of movement, not just the general idea. This is an exercise in observation, and you should change leaders without speaking.

4 This game can be played in a group. Stand in a circle. Without prior agreement, one person starts to move.

5 Those opposite this person "mirror," until the entire circle is engaged.

6 The object is to appear to move spontaneously, the group functioning as an organic whole, simultaneously creating the physical action.

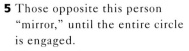

This exercise in making sounds also helps the group to work well together.

Sound Bath

The group lies on the floor on their backs, heads pointing to the center of a circle, feet at its circumference. All eyes are open and focused (but do not stare) at a point on the ceiling. One person sounds a note on "**MMMM**," and the others join in with harmonizing notes. Each person sings the note on a full exhalation, then chooses another harmonizing note. The object is to create a vibrating note from the full group that completely fills the room. The fullness of the sound must never diminish even though individuals are stopping and starting. When the sound is full on "**MMMMM**," individuals open their mouths on a vowel sound ("**MMMAAAA**!" or "**MMMMMEEEEEEE**!," for example) to create a fully expressive sound. See notes on Resonance (page 46) for a fuller explanation of this.

Exercise

Counting

The group counts to 20 and back to 1. No two people must speak at the same time. The object is to keep a light focused attention, and not to let the game disintegrate through frustration!

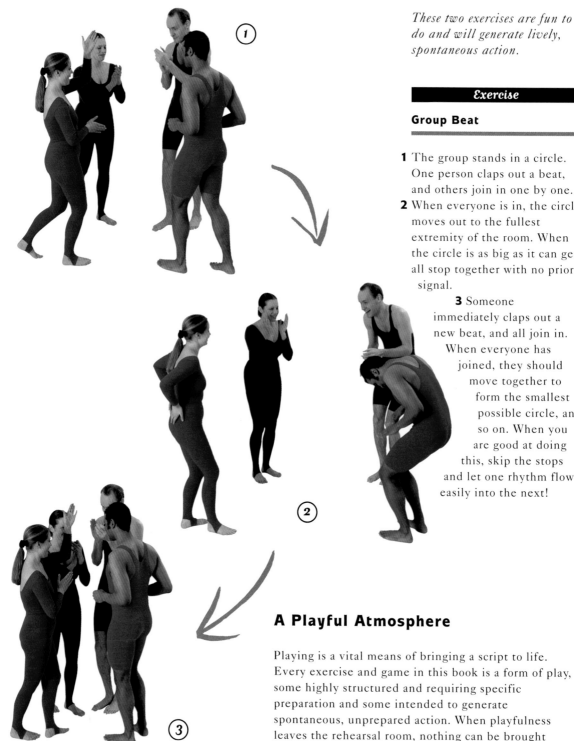

These two exercises are fun to do and will generate lively, spontaneous action.

Exercise

Group Beat

1 The group stands in a circle. One person claps out a beat, and others join in one by one.

2 When everyone is in, the circle moves out to the fullest extremity of the room. When the circle is as big as it can get, all stop together with no prior signal.

3 Someone immediately claps out a new beat, and all join in. When everyone has joined, they should move together to form the smallest possible circle, and so on. When you are good at doing this, skip the stops and let one rhythm flow easily into the next!

A Playful Atmosphere

Playing is a vital means of bringing a script to life. Every exercise and game in this book is a form of play, some highly structured and requiring specific preparation and some intended to generate spontaneous, unprepared action. When playfulness leaves the rehearsal room, nothing can be brought to life.

Exercise

Clown Play

1 Start in pairs. Clown 1 finds a
present. (Do not "think up" a
present. Let your hand or hands
fall on to, or find in the air, a
wrapped present.)

2 Clown 1 gives it to clown 2 who
instantly knows what the
present is.

3 Clown 2 uses it. It is the best
thing clown 2 has ever
received.

4 Clown 2 finds a present, and
gives it to clown 1, and so on.

5 In this game, each recipient of a
present is *ecstatic with joy*.
Anything less and the game does
not work.

6 Once the game is established,
more and more clowns can enter
with presents until there is an
orgy of present-giving. Or you
can play in pairs, and when the
energy is high, on a signal, break
into random present-giving. The
object is to establish and
maintain an atmosphere of
exuberant joy.

29

Chapter 2

The Actor's Instrument

Movement

An actor uses the body as an instrument. He or she does not train in the same way as, for example, an athlete. While fitness is essential both to the actor and the athlete, the actor must also develop an expressive body capable of "transformation."

Good actors come in all shapes and sizes, but whatever they look like they must be able to shift their center and adjust the weight, tempo and flow of their energy so as to create a range of different physical types. Mechanical exercises, which build muscle and stamina, do not in themselves develop in the actor a responsive and sensitive physical body – this comes instead from the imagination stimulating physical expression. Physical improvisation is therefore essential to bring to consciousness the "wholeness" of a physical action. Movement in acting begins with an imaginary impulse from the center and extends to the expressive periphery of the body as physical gesture, transforming and charging the surrounding space with energy.

The Spine

The spine is the expressive core of the body: the body's physical "signature." It directly transmits a person's energy, age, morale and state of tension. A flexible, free spine, uncharacterized by habitual misuse, is essential to the actor.

The spine consists of 33 small bones (vertebrae) which encase a stem of nerve tissue known as the spinal cord. This, and the brain, make up the central nervous system. The vertebrae at the base of the spine are fused. The others are separated by pads of cartilage, and are flexible. The whole consists of 7 neck vertebrae, 12 upper back vertebrae, 5 center back vertebrae and 9 "root" (fused) vertebrae.

Work on the spine is designed to free the flow of energy through the body and ease the tension knots that distort spinal posture and create secondary tensions in the body. Give special care to possible tension where the spine meets and balances the skull, which is the coordination center of the body. Also give special care to the point at which the flexible spine meets the fused vertebrae, which is the impulse or movement center of the body.

* *

Follow the instructions carefully and never try to manipulate the spine directly.

Exercise

An Aligned and Flexible Spine

1 First, stand on the ground! Place your feet about 1ft (30cm) apart. Imagine an axis from the middle of your heel to the pad of your big toe in each foot. Imagine a point at your little toe so that you can imagine you are balanced comfortably on two triangles. Drop to gravity – by this, I mean think "up"; don't collapse, but let gravity position your body without any resistant tensions. Do not lock your knees, elbows or wrists. Remember to continue to breathe!

Imagine your energy is pouring through your feet into the earth. Without doing anything, imagine your back broadening and widening, the top of your head tending to go up towards the ceiling, your chest and face radiating into the space. Focus on your breathing. Breathe out fully and let the in-breath take care of itself. Focus your attention towards any tightness or muscular "holding." If you find you are tired or tense, perhaps in your shoulder or leg, do not react physically. Don't fidget, but instead concentrate your mind upon the point of tension, and it will release itself. Practice will make you more accomplished at this. You will find that physical and psychological states often go together.

2 Open your eyes. Slowly let your head drop down, your chin on your chest, curling the neck (the first 7 vertebrae). Then curl the upper back (the next 12 vertebrae).

3 Finally, curl down the center (the lower 5 vertebrae). Remember that your knees are not locked.
Now uncurl from the base of the spine, one vertebra at a time. If you have a partner, get them to walk their fingers up your spine as you uncurl. Repeat 5 times.

See Salutation to the Sun on pages 18-19 for a dynamic spinal warm-up.

This should be done in pairs, and is a shake-out for the spine, shoulders and neck with one person massaging the other.

Exercise

A Flexible Spine Massage

1 The person to be massaged stands, and the "masseur" taps the other all over, gently shaking him or her out.

2 The person to be massaged stands and drops down from the waist. The knees are slightly flexible.
Make sure your partner is free at the neck and shoulders by gently moving them. Never manipulate the spine directly.

3 Rub gently on either side of the spinal column. Without touching the spine itself, warm up the lower back. Encourage your partner to give in to gravity, and let you move him or her around.

The spine should extend slightly as you work. Gently move the shoulders and gently move the head from side to side, working with your partner. Give in to the person who is moving you. The whole sequence should be very gentle and warming to the body. Do nothing that will jerk or jar the body. Never force anything as you move your partner. Speak to your partner.
Lightly massage the muscles at the back of the neck, making sure the head is free.

4 The person being massaged uncurls from the base of the spine. Do this *slowly*. Your partner walks their fingers up your spine as you uncurl. When the person is standing, lightly brush them down with your hands, to finish.

This is a back-to-back shake-out that should be done in pairs or groups.

Exercise

A Back-to-Back Shake-out

1 Position yourself carefully. Stand back to back. One person is going to take the other on his back, so that you are spine to spine. Follow the instructions carefully!

2 Link arms with your partner, but *do not pull them*. Carefully take your partner on your back and, as you slowly lean forward, your partner should lean back until they are lying on top of you. Note the position shown. You should both be very comfortable.

3 Unlink your arms so that you are balancing on each other. The person below now moves gently, the backs massaging each other.

The following exercise makes up, in its entirety, an excellent physical warm-up, and is fun to do.

Exercise

A Physical Warm-up

1 Stretch in a bubble. Move as though your body is enclosed in a bubble. First use your arms, then your arms and torso, and then your whole body, in all directions. Let the bubble be elastic and unbreakable!

2 Paint pot. Imagine that you have a large pot of paint. You dip your fingers in the pot, and flick away the paint. Use other parts of your body: your toes, elbows, arms and legs. Dip them in the pot and flick away the paint. Finish with a whole body-flick. Dip in your body and flick away!

3 Leg lifts. Swing the leg upward, and let the momentum lift you off the ground. Use one leg, then the other.

4 Run around and stop. The group moves lightly and quickly in the space. The group fills the whole area, and each individual moves into any available space on the floor. One member of the group claps (for example) and everyone is still, or sits. This continues for two or three minutes.

5 Neck and trunk curls. Let your head drop *gently* on to your chest and turn it *gently* to the right, to the back and around. Do this two or three times, and then two or three times in the opposite direction. Lean forward from your waist, swing *gently* to the right, to the back and around. Repeat two or three times, then repeat in the opposite direction.

6 Arm swings. Stand on the ground and bring your posture to mind. Swing one arm backwards in a circle. Keep a "level" energy; *don't strain the action*. Repeat with the other arm. Both arms work in a coordinated swing.

7 Steal the ribbons. Each player has ribbons tucked into the back of his or her waistband. Any number from one upward can be used. Players must try to steal other players' ribbons without allowing their own ribbons to be stolen. The player holding the most ribbons at the end "wins." The game helps the actor to gain a feeling of space through 360 degrees.

37

Posture

Most of us are unable to stand properly on the ground with an erect spine and with our bodies properly aligned, yet in early childhood our spines were practically straight. Psychological and physical misuse create tension points in the spine. To the actor, the most troublesome of these tension points are where the spine meets the base of the skull, and in the lumbar region where the flexible spine meets the fused part of the spine. Muscular tension is physical "holding" – a muscle that is constantly and restlessly at work. If this happens in the spinal region, other physical adjustments will have to be made, such as movement in the head or locking the knees, to stop you falling over. Thus a complicated pattern of tensions pulls the body out of alignment. This is Feldenkrais's definition of good posture, which is particularly relevant to the actor.

The proper posture of the body is such that:

- It can initiate movement in any direction with the same ease.

- It can start any movement without a preliminary adjustment.

- It can move with the minimum of work, i.e. the maximum of efficiency.

Good posture is not achieved by "doing." Doing only reinforces bad habits. Bring your own posture to consciousness. Do not imitate the military "ramrod" posture. This is *entirely wrong* for you. Say to yourself, "I am standing tall. My spine is lengthening and my back is widening; my neck is free. Energy is flowing through my ankles, wrists, elbows, knees, hips . . . . I am still, but I could move at any time." Sooner or later, your body will do what it is told, on its own. Make these instructions your preparation for your physical and vocal work.

A military "holding" style of posture.

"My spine is lengthening and my back is widening; my neck is free."

A curved spine and collapsed chest.

The Physical Center

The physical center is located in the middle of your solar plexus. It is from here that all physical and vocal impulses emanate, so it is worth taking time to locate it. Its position may shift according to your mood and circumstance. It is not purely mechanical – the center is a psychophysical phenomenon and must be "sensed" rather than physically located. That said, your center is certainly not in your chest or throat, and it is almost certainly lower down than you suspect!

This exercise will help you to align yourself properly and find your center.

Exercise

Locating the Center

1 Align yourself as in the Aligned and Flexible Spine exercise on page 32.

2 Rock backward and forward. Rotate three or four times, focusing on your center. Come to rest.

3 Place your feet a yard (meter) apart and sway gently from side to side. Come to rest, lightly directing your attention to the center. Remind yourself that your wrists, elbows, shoulders, knees and ankles are released and not locked. Say to yourself, "I could move if I wanted to, but at this moment I choose not to."

Now allow yourself to move, but move from the center. Let every movement be powered by a flow of energy from the center. How would you characterize the energy? Does it flow strongly through you, or seep slowly, or rage through you? Is it light or heavy? Quick or slow? Try altering some of these variables.

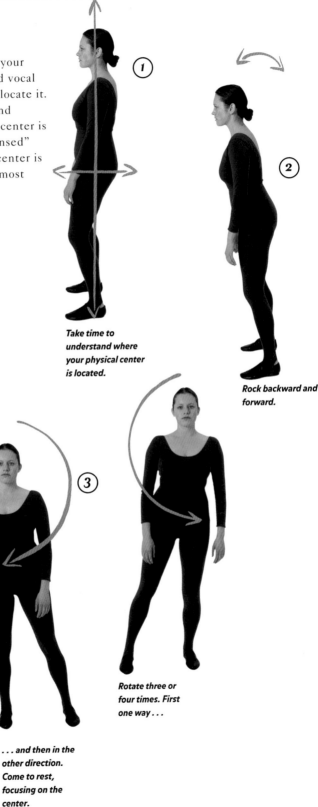

Take time to understand where your physical center is located.

Rock backward and forward.

Rotate three or four times. First one way . . .

. . . and then in the other direction. Come to rest, focusing on the center.

Physical Presence

"Presence" has to do with what you *are*, not with what you *do*. The more you strive to create presence, the smaller you become. Nevertheless, it is possible to cultivate presence, firstly by developing a sensitive physical body, secondly by directing and focusing your energy until to do so becomes second nature.

Exercise

Filling the Space

Move into the working space, bringing to your consciousness the size of the space, the walls and corners and features of the room. Tell yourself you are going to fill this space with yourself. Start from a crouched position and gradually unfold. Powered by the center, make a series of expansive movements, and open yourself as wide as you can. When your body is fully open, don't "lock" it. Imagine that the energy flows from your center through your arms and legs, through your toes and fingers and into the space, so you feel that you extend into the space, and that you actually get larger.

Hold the expanded moment for some time. Enjoy the sensation! Create some bold, expansive gestures using the same sense of energy flow into the space, saying as you do them, "strong and free!" Fling an imaginary object into a corner of the room, letting your

energy, impelled from the center, stream past your fingertips. Use your whole body. In the same way, make an expansive bow to the wall, pick up an imaginary bulky object, lift it high and fling it into the space.

Don't "act" any of this simple, psychophysical work. Imagine your legs and arms are attached not to your shoulders and hips but directly to the center. Fling yourself into a chair, your body wide open. Be still. Imagine that you radiate into the space, that the entire room is filled up with your energy. Do nothing. When you have filled the space, imagine that the walls fall away, exposing an infinitely massive imaginary space. Imagine that energy is drawn from the earth through your feet, radiating from the entire surface of your body, into the space. Do nothing.

This exercise will encourage you to understand physical presence in the space around you.

Exercise

Discovering Physical Presence

1 Moving from your center, engage your whole body in an action that "expands" your body into the space around you. Continue to breathe; do not "tense" into the space, but release yourself. When you have reached maximum physical size without stress or tension, imagine that your energy continues to flow into the space through the tips of your fingers. Continue to draw up energy from the earth through your feet. Let it flow through you into the room. Imagine that you continue to increase in size. Practice with different energy impulses: slow and languishing sensation or flaring sensation, and so on.

①

Let your body expand to its fullest extent. Imagine that you continue to expand through your toes and fingertips.

②

Your body begins to suck energy from the room.

From the open position, imagine that your body is sucking energy from the room. Let it flow through your fingers, into your body and away into the earth, until there's nothing left in the room.

2 Let it remove your bodily energy so that you begin to implode, as if there is nothing inside you.

3 Feel yourself crumple; if someone touched you, you would shatter or turn to dust. Imagine you have vaporized into the room. Then draw up energy as before.

③

You feel yourself crumple. Then draw up energy, until you reach step 1 again.

Physical Transformation

Work on the basic orientation exercises before you go on to the transformation exercises that follow. You must be able to stand with good posture and free energy before you begin to characterize.

In this exercise you endow the space around you with specific qualities.

Exercise

Earth, Water, Air and Fire

When you "endow" a space, a prop or a person, you act toward them as though they had certain specific qualities you have chosen for them in your imagination. You could endow a person as a block of ice, or a sweet-scented rose, or an ice-cream that you wanted to eat (see also Imaginative Warm-ups on pages 20-1). For the moment, I want you to endow the space in the following ways, using the elements of earth, water, air and fire.

Earth. Imagine that the room you are standing in is a block of solid substance, and that when you move, you are cutting through this substance. Stand in the room and, from your center, begin to move your arms and legs, making simple, broad, pleasurable gestures which cut and mold the air. In your imagination, keep the air thick, substantial and not too resistant. You will find that your gestures seem very deliberate and that each move has a beginning, a middle and an end. Don't "act" any of this. Concentrate on imaginatively transforming the space. The physical action should have a psychological effect on you. Don't think too much about it, but be aware of it. Remember the initial sensations. The resistance is not so severe that you are "moonwalking!" You simply allow the resistance to affect the weight and flow of your gestures.

Earth

Invent a small, realistic *movement*.

Scenario. For example, you enter the room and sit down at a table. You are waiting for someone. He or she is late. You look at your watch. You become anxious and pace the floor. You stop, hear a noise! It's them! You prepare yourself – your hair, your clothes. You listen. Nothing. You open the door: nothing. End.

Use this little pattern of activities, or another of your own invention, to practice moving from the center in the space endowed as I suggest in the exercise, using either earth, water, air or fire movements. You create both *external* movements and *internal* impulses, which power the movements. Now you must balance the realism of the scenario with the movement characteristics. You will have to find the correct balance by *internalizing* some of the activity. How much of the molding movement you show will depend on the style of the scene.

What sort of person are you creating? Use a prop or a simple piece of costume if it helps.

Water. Start the sequence again from the beginning, but this time imagine that the "substance" which fills the room bears you up and supports you. As you move in the room, let your movements flow one into the other. Do not "dance." Endow the space with this quality and let it affect the way you move. The "space substance" moves easily around you and inside you, ebbing and flowing. When you have explored this in an abstract way, using your whole body and moving from the center, invent a scenario and play it as before. Experiment with tempo. How does the energy flow from the center? Does it seep through you, flow or gush? Use images of flowing water in a river: rapids, still, deep pools or strong, steady flow. What sort of person is emerging?

Water

Air. The "space substance" that fills the room in this case is so light that all gestures continue in the space indefinitely. There is no resistance to your movements and you take pleasure in their sustained, light quality. Endow your center with airy qualities so that your movements are urged by an air stream or a blast of air, or an explosion. Don't act, or you will predict the outcome and end up with a string of clichés. It is vital in these exercises that you "explore." Play a movement scenario as before. What character is emerging?

Air

Fire. In this improvisation the "space substance" (the endowed air) is yourself. You radiate into the space, filling it with your heat. Avoid muscular tension in all of these exercises. Imagine, as you make a movement, that there is a slight afterburn trailing behind it. When you stop, let energy continue to radiate from your center into the space. Fill the entire room with your energy, as you did when exploring stage presence. Create a small movement scenario as before. What sort of character is emerging?

Fire

When exploring these four states, begin with abstract gestures to get a sense of the dynamic of the movements. Each state suggests a whole range of movement. When you come to the movement scenarios, which are more realistic, note the psychological sensations which emerge as you work. Does the movement make you feel joyful, determined, vulnerable, powerful, radiant? Movement for actors is psychophysical. Let the gesture evoke sensation, and let this sensation evoke and inform subsequent gestures.

Fire

Fire

Elements of Effort

Rudolph Laban (1879–1958), the Hungarian choreographer and dance theorist, created a training system for dancers in his analysis of movement as effort and action. This system is frequently adapted to actor training both to explore the total expressive range of the actor's body and to create characters physically. In this section, which deals with movement improvisation, we shall explore different combinations of effort and action.

Laban defined four movement elements that can be combined in different variations:

- The element of *weight* in movement is characterized at one end of the spectrum as *firm, contending* and *strongly resistant*, and at the other as *gentle, indulgent* and *weakly resistant*.

- The element of *time* in movement is characterized at one extreme as *sudden, broken* and *quick*, and at the other as *sustained, indulgent* and *slow*.

- The element of *space* in movement is characterized by actions that are, on the one hand, *direct, contending* and in a *straight line* and, on the other hand, by actions that are *flexible, indulgent* and *turning*.

- The element of *energy flow* at one extreme is *bound, holding* and *contending*, and at the other is *free, releasing* and *indulgent*.

Explore the following action shapes by combining elements.

Exercise

Exploring Action Shapes

Move in a way which is:

Firm, DIRECT, *sustained*.

Then change one element:

Gentle, DIRECT, *sustained*.

Then change one element:

Gentle, indirect, *sustained*.

Then change one element:

Firm, indirect, *sustained*.

Then change one element:

Firm, indirect, *S U D D E N*.

Then change one element:

Gentle, indirect, *S U D D E N*.

Then change one element:

Gentle, DIRECT, *S U D D E N*.

Then change one element:

Firm, DIRECT, *S U D D E N*.

Exercise

Exploring Movement Factors

Explore the movement factors of weight, time, space and flow, one factor at a time. Concentrate first on the *contrast* between the two extremes in each category, feeling the difference in your body. Then focus on the *spectrum* in each category, moving by degrees from one extreme to the other.

Firm, DIRECT, *sustained*.
(Pressing)

Gentle, DIRECT, *sustained*.
(Gliding)

These are the eight basic effort actions. You can explore each one using *bound* (controlling, stopping) energy or *free* (releasing, fluent) energy. Some combinations will lend themselves more to free or to bound energy. Some combinations will allow both.

Gentle, indirect, *sustained*.
(Floating)

Firm, DIRECT, *SUDDEN*.
(Punching)

Firm, indirect, *sustained*.
(Wringing)

Gentle, DIRECT, *SUDDEN*.
(Dabbing)

Gentle, indirect, *SUDDEN*.
(Flicking)

Firm, indirect, *SUDDEN*.
(Slashing)

45

Voice

Treat your voice exactly as though it were a musical instrument. Show a similar respect for it by keeping it in superb condition and practicing frequently.

As **with** an instrument, "little and often" is the rule for practice. Twenty minutes *every* day is better than an hour when you can fit it in. Take pleasure in your work. Enjoy your capacity to expand your ribcage, to fill your lungs with air and to create sound. Your pleasure in the work is an important aspect of it. If you feel a little uncertain or awkward with the exercises at first, persevere! Try them out for a period of time and see what happens. Remember that this is part of an extended process. Building practice into your daily routine is the surest way to develop your voice.

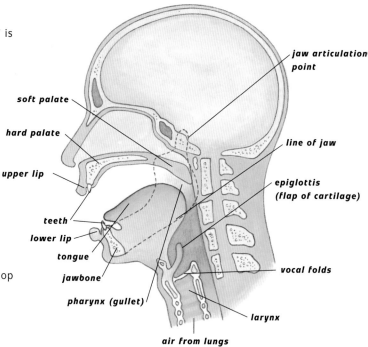

soft palate
hard palate
upper lip
teeth
lower lip
tongue
jawbone
pharynx (gullet)
jaw articulation point
line of jaw
epiglottis (flap of cartilage)
vocal folds
larynx
air from lungs

How Sound is Produced

Before you practice, you should know how the voice works. Sound is made by vibrating air. Vocal sound is created when a stream of air passes over the *vocal folds*, which are located in the throat, behind the Adam's apple. These folds used to be called vocal cords, but they are, in fact, folds of muscle. The stream of air is produced by the lungs, but it is of the utmost importance that the stream of air is centered and controlled. This is done by the *diaphragm*, a sheet of muscle that separates the chest from the abdomen. Sound thus produced is made louder by *resonators*, which are cavities in the body. Mouth, throat and nasal resonators can be controlled and used in the production of sound.

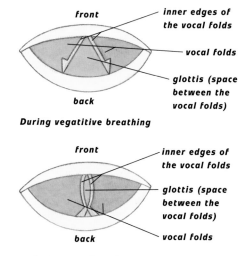

front
inner edges of the vocal folds
vocal folds
glottis (space between the vocal folds)
back

During vegetative breathing

front
inner edges of the vocal folds
glottis (space between the vocal folds)
back
vocal folds

During sound production

How to Breathe

The breathing we do to stay alive, called *vegetative breathing*, is very different from that used for sound production. Vegetative breathing, and that used for casual conversation, is usually *thoracic*, which means that when you inhale, the chest expands and the stomach retracts. The shoulders, collarbone and breastbone are engaged. This sometimes creates tensions around the throat that are not noticed in conversation but which impede and create strain when an energized, sustained and projected voice is required. To do the work of an actor, you must breathe from the *diaphragm*.

This exercise shows you how to breathe properly from the diaphragm.

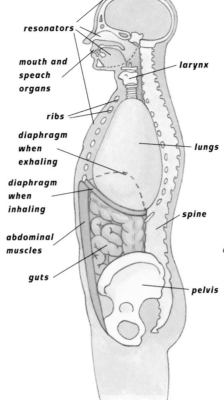

resonators

mouth and speach organs

ribs

diaphragm when exhaling

diaphragm when inhaling

abdominal muscles

guts

larynx

lungs

spine

pelvis

Do some press-ups, or sit-ups, or enough exercise to make you out of breath. You are now breathing from your diaphragm. Put your hand on your stomach and notice that it expands against your hand when you inhale. Your neck and shoulders are free. Breathing from the diaphragm is what the body does naturally when it needs to ventilate efficiently. It is a natural form of breathing; you must cultivate and practice it because it is the foundation of a good voice and clear speech, and essential for vocal projection.

Exercise

Breathing from the Diaphragm

Lie down somewhere comfortable and warm. Use the position suggested on page 14 if you wish. Without actual movement or fidgeting, tell your shoulders to do nothing and tell your back to broaden and widen. Concentrate on your exhalation without "doing." Let the inhalation take care of itself.

Place a book on your stomach. Let the book rise as the inhalation takes place, and return to its original position when you exhale. Vocalize on "Ahhh." Do not "do" anything;' let it happen.

Stand up, put a hand on your

stomach, stick out your tongue and pant like a dog. When you breathe in, your stomach moves out. Practice slowly until you have the action of the diaphragm.

Stand on the ground, feet apart. Lift your heels a little and drop back on to your feet. Feel the slight jolt. Repeat this, making the sound "Ha" as you drop to your heels. Let the tiny jolt produce the sound. Bounce lightly on your heels, producing "Ha . . . Ha . . . Ha . . . ." Drop to your heels and produce "Haaaaaaaaaaaaaaa!" Your shoulders and neck are free; use only breaths from the diaphragm.

Stand with your feet apart; then lift your heels. Say "Ha" as you drop back to your heels.

Relaxing the Voice

A voice produced from a relaxed throat is more pleasant to listen to, and is easier to sustain. A relaxed speaking voice is superior to the casual conversational voice (with its variety of tensions) for the following reasons:

- It is easier to project a relaxed voice.

- A relaxed voice is easier to control in terms of volume and speed of delivery. More variation is therefore possible.

- Usually the pitch of the voice drops when the throat is relaxed. It is more easily heard and therefore more easily understood.

There is no point in dealing with problems of articulation if the voice remains tense. This is why release, centering and relaxation are basic preparations for voice work (the exercises described on pages 14–15 and 16–17 can be used as preparation).

A basic relaxation exercise for the throat.

Exercise

Creating an Open Throat

First, exercise to free your shoulders and neck. Bring your shoulders up around your ears. Let the shoulders drop. Drop them more. Step up the shoulders alternately to the count of 20. Drop the shoulders. Bring the shoulders towards your ears. Rotate them backward and up. Reverse the rotation. Release your shoulders.

Bring up your shoulders to your ears.

Step up the shoulders alternately.

Let your head fall toward your chest. Rotate your head *very gently* to the side, back and around to your chest. Repeat three or four times, then reverse the rotation.

Get the feel of an "open throat" by yawning. Slowly draw in air while opening the back of your throat. Really yawn. Leave your shoulders alone! If the action makes you want to stretch, do it. As you yawn, begin to vocalize. Say, "I am speaking with an open throat" as you yawn.

Exercise

Breath Control

Taking a breath from the diaphragm, and, using an open throat, make a pre-vocal sound. The sound should be like the clicking of a Geiger counter. Allow the flow of breath to increase until a note is *just* produced. Increase the volume of sound to the end of the exhalation. Explore simple patterns using a single exhalation; for instance, strong note to quiet, to pre-vocal, to strong. Tell yourself that your shoulders are not required for this, and place a hand on your stomach immediately below your sternum (breastbone) making sure that it continues to expand on the in-breath (a diaphragm breath).

Rotate your head.

Yawn.

The Vocal Center and Diaphragm

The vocal center is about three-fingers' width below the navel.

The vocal center lies in the middle of the body.

Hands should be placed just below the lower ribs. Cough gently to get the feeling of the diaphragm expanding. Now go through the alphabet. Speak each letter six times.

Vocal Balancing

If you are working with an actor friend, or in a group, try these balancing exercises. You release the sound when you feel in perfect balance with your partner.

①

In this exercise you balance facing your partner.

Exercise

Blind Balancing

1 Face your partner. Standing about 1 yard (1 meter) from your partner, grip each other's wrists, so you have a firm but not "hard" grip.

2 Lean backward so that you are taking your partner's weight. Remember that you can bend your knees! Even if you and your partner are different weights, you can balance by one going lower than the other, like a seesaw. This is not a

In this exercise you have your backs against each other.

Exercise

Back to Back

1 Sit on the ground with your back to your partner so that you are back to back. Link arms.

2 Push yourselves up gently, moving together, until you are in a balanced position. You should not be standing, but balanced against your partner's back, so if you moved away, your partner would fall over.

3 Vocalize. Use vowels; concentrate on *resonance*. Make your backs vibrate together! Release your arms, and let your head rest on the other's shoulder. Be relaxed and in balance.

gymnastic exercise. There is no position you "must" achieve, but it is important to work according to the capacity of your partner.

3 You can move up and down, together or as a seesaw, but make sure you have your partner's weight all the time. When you both feel secure with this, begin to vocalize. Vocalize on "**MMMMM**" or "**NNNNN**" or **NNNGGGG**."

4 When you have established a good sound together, open your mouths to make "**MMMMAAAAAA**!" Let this happen together between you, and without any prior signal so that in this exercise you are sensing each other throughout.

Vocal Warm-up

Vocal warm-ups are ideal to get your voice into good "working order." You should practice moving and making sounds at the same time, as well as using the body's resonators (where sound vibrates).

SHHHHH!

This vocal warm-up takes 15 minutes.

3

HA! HA! HA!

2

YAWN

1

5 Squat down, with your feet flat on the ground. Breathe in and vocalize on "**SHHHHhhhhh**!" Imagine that the sound comes through your crotch.

6 Start to roll the hips, moving into a shake-out. Release sound as you do this. Don't force the sound; let it happen.

7 Practice throwing and catching sounds. Let your movements be powered from the center, and release the sound with the movement. Vary the physical throws, and vary the range of sounds with the range of throws and catches.

Exercise

Movement, Sound and Resonance

1 Yawning, stretch out slowly, open your throat and yawn. Don't "act" this, but really try to make it happen.

2 Allow yourself to laugh. Release the laugh, but don't force it. Feel the "Ha! Ha! Ha!" move the diaphragm. This helps you to place your voice.

3 Push your tongue out and down as far as it will go. Pant on the diaphragm.

4 Raise your arm up, and lift it over to your left. Think "up and over." Work to the left and to the right. This moves and warms up the lower ribs.

OOOH!

OUCH!

7

8 Practice a siren sound. Let yourself curl down until you hang from the waist. As you *gently* curl down, release a sound that rises in pitch as you go down and drops in pitch as you come up. This sound is like a rising and falling siren.

⑧

WHOOO!

Head

Face mask, temples, cheeks, nasal resonators

⑨

Upper chest

9 Practice resonance. Vocalize a sound using the sounds "**MMMMMMMMM**!" or "**NNNNNNNN**!" Don't force the sound. The purpose of this exercise is to allow the body to resonate (vibrate). Check that all of the resonators – the cavities in your head and body – are functioning as you continue to make your sound. For example, put your hand on your head to feel the vibration.

Lower back and torso

10 Practice sending sounds into space. Resonate on "**MMMMM**!" or "**NNNNN**!" with closed lips, then open your arms, open your body and open your lips with a vowel sound that fills the space. Always finish by speaking a piece of text.

MMMMMM!

⑩

53

Speech

Speech is about communication. The words you say must be clearly articulated, spoken with focused, vital energy and projected precisely toward their object. The inner key to all this is "intention." You have to really want to communicate and what you say has to be important. Without this underpinning desire, all the technique in the world is useless.

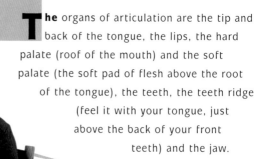

The organs of articulation are the tip and back of the tongue, the lips, the hard palate (roof of the mouth) and the soft palate (the soft pad of flesh above the root of the tongue), the teeth, the teeth ridge (feel it with your tongue, just above the back of your front teeth) and the jaw.

Speech consists broadly of two categories of sound-making: consonants and vowels.

Your intention and your desire to communicate are as important as articulation in the creation of clear speech.

Speech should always be clearly articulated . . .

Consonants

Consonants are sounds made when the passage of air over the vocal folds is stopped or obstructed in some way.

There are two types of consonant sound. The first, exploding or "plosive" consonants, are made by stopping the air completely, then releasing sound as the air is released – a little explosion. Try p, *t*, *k*, **CH**. Place your fingers in front of your mouth as you speak them. These are strong plosives. There are weaker plosives: *b*, *d*, G. Feel the difference in plosive power between the two types. Sound is exploded variously using the lips, tongue tip, tongue and soft palate. Explore these different sounds.

The second type of consonants are "continuants," which means that the passage of air is only partly blocked so the consonant can be "breathed" as well as voiced.

Try m, *n* and **NG** (for the last, place the back of the tongue on the soft palate). The lips and tongue block the air passage through the mouth, but air still passes through the nose.

Try *l* and *r* in which the tongue tip creates a precise obstruction in the mouth, but air continues to pass between the lips.

The last group of continuants are best understood in pairs, one breathed and one voiced. Try the following: *th* (as in thin – breathed) and **TH** (as in that – voiced). Then try *ss* (breathed) and **ZZ** (voiced), *f* (breathed) and **V** (voiced).

. . . and projected precisely toward the person.

First, some tongue twisters that will help you practice articulation of consonants.

Exercises

Articulation of Consonants

I never felt felt
feel flat like
that felt felt.

Red Lorry,
Yellow Lorry,
Red Lorry,
Yellow Lorry.

Many men many men many men men men!
Many men many men many men men men!
Many men many men many men men men!
Many men! Many men men men!
(To the tune of the *William Tell Overture*)

Peter Piper picked a peck
of pickled peppers,
A peck of pickled peppers
Peter Piper picked.

Fanny Finch fried
five flounders for
Francis Fowler's
father.

She sells seashells
by the seashore.

Gilbert and Sullivan are an endless source of articulation exercises.
Try this:

You must lie upon the daisies and discourse in novel phrases of your complicated state of mind,
The meaning doesn't matter if it's only idle chatter of a transcendental kind.
    And everyone will say,
    As you walk your mystic way,
"If this young man expresses himself in terms too deep for *me*,
Why, what a very singularly deep young man this deep young man must be!"
(From *Patience* by Gilbert and Sullivan)

Speak the following carefully and slowly, beginning and ending your words, feeling the shifts of tongue, teeth and lips. Then speak with flow and expression.

Between two hawks, which flies the higher pitch;
Between two dogs, which hath the deeper mouth;
Between two blades; which bears the better temper;
Between two horses, which doth bear him best;
Between two girls, which hath the merriest eye –
I have, perhaps, some shallow spirit of judgement;
But in these nice sharp quillets of the law,
Good faith, I am no wiser than a daw.
(From *Henry VI, Part One* by William Shakespeare)

Vowels

Vowels are opposite to consonants. A vowel is a free, unobstructed flow of vibrating breath. It is always continuant and always voiced. There are five vowels: A, E, I, O, U; but there are many more vowel sounds which can be made, shaped by the lips, the tongue and the jaw.

This exercise will help you to practice the articulation of vowels.

Exercise

Articulation of Vowels

Using mainly the lips, explore the following "front vowels":

wE sHAll mAkE thEm Ill At lAst

Exaggerate the movements of the lips to make the vowel sounds "muscular." Lengthen and fully shape the sounds.

As before, use the tongue and lips to explore these "middle vowels."

Up furthEr...! fUrther!

Exaggerate and feel the sounds as before. Now use the tongue and the jaw for the back vowels:

cArl wAnts All Old bOOks tOO

There are also combinations of vowel sounds called diphthongs (two sounds together). Try these diphthongs:

mAY I jOIn YOU nOW jOE?

Exaggerate as before. Feel the way one vowel sound glides into another. (Y and W count as vowels here.)

Now practice both consonants and vowels.

Exercise

For Consonants and Vowels

Use the following passage from Shakespeare's *Measure for Measure* Act 2, Scene 2, line 112. Read it through exaggerating and shaping the consonants. Then read it through again, exaggerating the vowel sounds.

The letters in capitals should be emphasized.

Isabella:
Could GReat Men THuNDer
aS JoVe hiMSeLF DoeS, JoVe
woulD NeVer Be QUieT,
For eVeRy PeLTiNG PeTTy oFFiCer
woulD uSE hiS heaVen For THuNDer,
NoTHiNG BuT THuNDeR!

First read through and feel the weight of the consonants, as though the consonants themselves were falling from heaven, thudding, shattering and stinging the earth as they fall.

Now imagine that Isabella is spitting at Angelo, using enormous variety, drawing spittle from every part of her mouth! Look up the speech and do the whole of it like this!

Now read again, carefully shaping the vowels.

cOUld grEAt mEn thUndEr
As jOve HImsElf dOEs, jOve
WOUld nEvEr bE quIEt,
fOr EverY pEltIng pEttY OffIcEr
WOUld Use HIs HEAven fOr thUndEr,
nOthIng bUt thUndEr!

Read it again as though Isabella is crying, or expressing pain.

Projection

Projection involves *intention* and *focus*. A common error is to try to achieve projection through volume and pitch. This invariably results in stress and "pushing." Use the following exercise to develop your ability to "place" the voice.

This will help you to project into the space around you.

Exercise

Projection

Find a large room – the larger, the better for most voice work. Outside is fine if you can maintain concentration in the face of bemused passersby! Focus on two points in the distance, and two in the middle distance. Let them be distributed about the room. Place a chair next to you. This is your "confidant." You are going to "place" your voice far, middle and close (to the chair).

Stand on the floor and prepare yourself vocally. Lift yourself on to your toes, and as you come down on your heels, throw a vowel sound: "Ah!" or "Ha!" or "Oh!, " etc., at one of your chosen points in the distance. Let the point be specific. Repeat this action, throwing the sound from the center, using your whole body. Throw with your arm, powered by the center. Throw to the distance, pitch accurately to the mid-distance and toss gently into the chair, without altering pitch or volume as you throw the sound, and tell yourself to "follow through. You *place* your voice by *focus* and *intention*.

In this exercise, use the far, middle and close points as in the last exercise.

Exercise

Placing the Voice

Place your voice in the far distance when speaking the sections in ordinary type. Underlined sections are placed to the middle distance and sections in parentheses are placed to the chair. Do not vary the volume as you change placings. When you have practiced and accomplished the exercise with flow, focus and panache, bow! (A certain extravagance is permitted in speech work!)

Focus on specific points in the far distance. Pitch your voice to these points.

Again the violet of our early days
Drinks beauteous Azure from the golden sun,
And kindles into fragrance at his blaze;
<u>The streams, rejoiced that winter's work is done,</u>
<u>Talk of tomorrow's cowslips as they run,</u>
Wild apple, thou art burstling into bloom!
Thy leaves are coming, snowy blossomed thorn!
(Wake, buried lily! spirit quit thy tomb;
And thou, shade-loving hyacinth, be born!)
<u>Then haste, sweet rose! sweet woodbine, hymn the morn,</u>
<u>Whose dewdrops shall illume with pearly light</u>
Each grassy blade that thick embattled stands
From sea to sea (while daisies infinite
Uplift in praise their little glowing hands),
O'er every hill that under heaven stands.

"Spring" by Ebenezer Elliot (1781–1849)

Choose specific points in the middle distance. Pitch your voice accurately to these points.

Pitch your voice close to the chair or a person sitting in it. Toss the sound gently and precisely to this point.

Speech Warm-up

The following exercises make up an ideal speech warm-up.

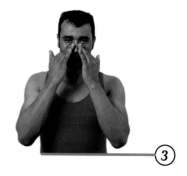

You should start with a face massage.

Face Massage

1 First, massage the scalp (the head resonators).
2 Second, massage the temples.
3 Then massage the side of the nose (the nasal resonators).
4 Next, massage the axis of the jaw (to get the jaw relaxed). Stroke down, loosen and relax the jaw.
5 Check that your jaw is relaxed by placing two fingers in your mouth.
6 Warm up the muscles at the back of your neck.
7 Gently massage the point where the head balances on the spine.

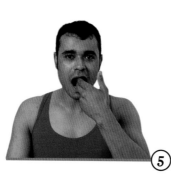

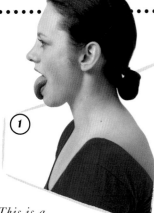

(1)

This is a warm-up for the muscles of the tongue.

Exercise

Tongue Muscles

1 Out and down . . .
2 . . . and up.
3 Extend the tongue and roll the tip around.
4 Curl the tongue. Lift the tip of the tongue firmly to touch the ridge just behind the front teeth.

(2)

(3)

(4)

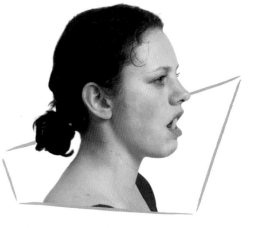

A bone prop can be useful.

Exercise

Using a Bone Prop

The bone prop is a small plastic rod, which is used to prop open the mouth while warming up the lips and tongue. You can use any safe and clean piece of plastic or cork, placed between the front teeth. It must be not longer than 1in (2.5cm). Make sure that your neck stays free and that you don't push your head forward during these exercises. A simple mental reminder before the exercise should suffice.

Say "lah," letting the tongue drop fully to behind the lower teeth. Repeat with "lah lah, lah, lah," and then "lahlahlahlah," making firm and full use of the tongue with each "lah." Repeat for "tah," "dah" and "nah." Hold the consonant firmly for a second and release the "ah" as you let the tongue drop fully. Remember to release the sound rather than push it out. Still using the prop, warm up the lips with "pah," "mah" and "bah." You can extend the exercise to "pahpahpah," etc.

Practice your vowel sounds.

A Vowel Sequence

This sequence is called the figure of eight. Enjoy the sensation of molding the airstream to create a progression of vowel shapes. Let the shape light up your entire face.

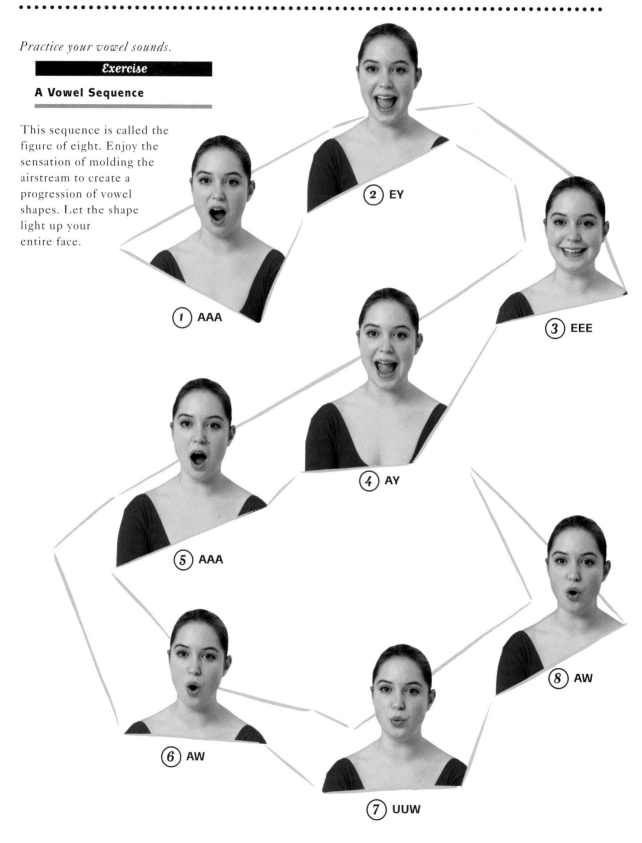

① AAA

② EY

③ EEE

④ AY

⑤ AAA

⑥ AW

⑦ UUW

⑧ AW

PAH!

EEEE!

AAA!

Use both vowels and consonants in the following exercise.

Exercise

Shoot the Arrow

A vocalized vowel is made as the arm comes over to take the string ("Aaaaaaa!," "Eeeeeee!," "Iiiiii!," "Ooooooo!," "Uuuuuuu!") and a plosive consonant is sounded on release of the string ("Pah!," "Dah!," "Kah!").

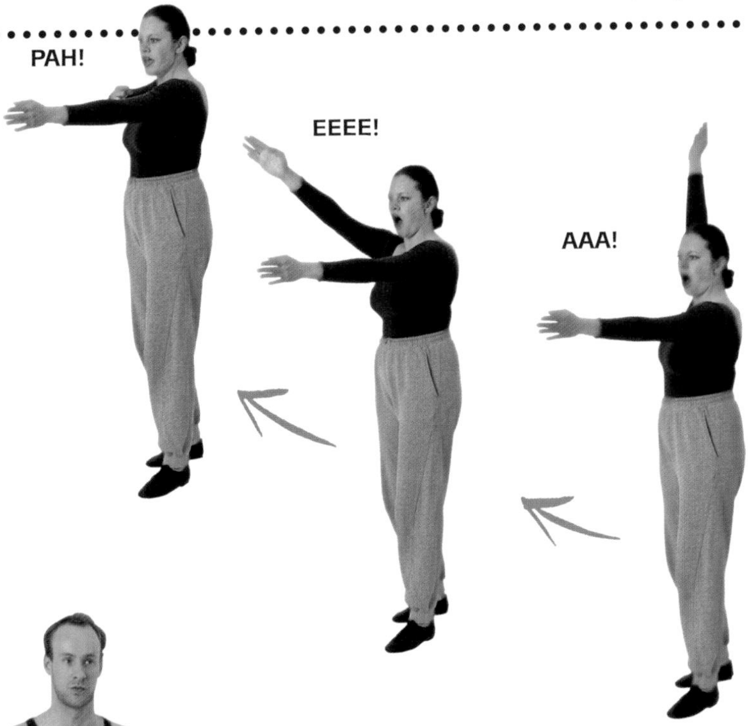

①

②

③

Finish with some text.

Exercise

Physical Expression

Experiment to create a physical expression for each beat of the text. In this example, the idea of melting flesh is made physical so that the words are able to literally "move" the actor.

1 "Oh, that this too too solid flesh . . ."
2 ". . . would melt . . ."
3 ". . . thaw. . ."
4 ". . . and resolve itself into dew."

④

63

Chapter 3

The Actor in Rehearsal

The Rehearsal Process

It is most important that you use every scrap of the rehearsal process to understand your part in the production and to communicate with everyone else who is involved.

It is easy to say this and hard to do because you can easily fall into the fallacy that "we haven't really started yet," "we're just reading through" or "we're not off the book yet." Sloppy directors support this misguided view, and you will rapidly find yourself in a situation where, although rehearsals are taking place, no actual work is being done. It is the actor's job to keep open the process of exploration, and not to "shut down," relieved, once the first decisions have been taken. This does not mean you avoid making choices. You must make clear choices through the entire rehearsal process, but remain flexible, and don't be afraid to discard your work.

All actors work differently. Some seem to grasp everything very quickly, then "go off." They can't develop or even recapture what they did early in rehearsal, and they are unable to let go of what they found initially. Other actors turn in work very late, and directors complain that the actor "can't rehearse." Fellow actors then feel let down in rehearsal. Yet other actors experience a severe crisis of confidence during the rehearsal process, without which they can't in fact turn in a good performance. As you gain experience, learn to observe your patterns. You will never solve them completely, but you will learn to understand them. Remember that theatre is a social art and therefore it is necessary, from time to time, to communicate to others what is happening to you.

You also have certain professional responsibilities. You are responsible for your own work, for your choices and for the clarity of your work. It is your job to turn up to work on time, having prepared yourself and done whatever homework you have agreed with the director. You are not to give way to artistic temperament or tantrums. This is the preserve of rank amateurs and stars. You must think through problems, rather than become bogged down with them. Take a positive attitude and be good to work with!

Rehearsal is a cooperative process, but each individual also experiences his or her own rehearsal pattern.

The Production Process

At the center of the production process is the

DIRECTOR

who chooses the **PLAY** and imagines a world in which the play will be brought to life.

The Director **AUDITIONS** the

ACTORS

who form a

COMPANY

who work under the supervision of the Director to realize the concept in terms of script interpretation and character development.

The Director explains the **CONCEPT** of the play to the

DESIGNER

who conceives these ideas in terms of acting space, color, shape and scale. This is the **SET**.

The Designer works with the

COSTUME DESIGNER

LIGHTING DESIGNER

SOUND TECHNICIAN

to realize **PHYSICALLY** the world of the play, always referring to the Director.

The Director agrees a practical work schedule with the

PRODUCTION MANAGER

who calls **PRODUCTION MEETINGS** with the Director, Designer and the

STAGE MANAGER

who obtains the **PROPS**, creates a **PROMPT COPY** and assists rehearsal with the help of the

DEPUTY STAGE MANAGER

ASSISTANT STAGE MANAGER.

The Director works in rehearsal with the Company, in small groups or individuals as required. Actors are "**CALLED**" on **REHEARSAL SCHEDULES**.

Production meetings start to involve the design team, the **STAGE CREW** who will run the show, and the construction team, including the **CARPENTER** and **ELECTRICIAN**.

The Production team work with the Designer to construct what has been agreed with the Director. They meet regularly with the Director.

Rehearsals increasingly involve props, practical parts of the set and practice costumes.

The Production Manager organizes the whole production team (Designers to Crew) towards the "**GET IN**" or "**FIT UP**." Either term means to set up the show physically in the theatre.

The Director then **PLOTS** the levels and cues for lighting and sound with the Lighting Designer and the Sound Technician. Actors appear at the "**TECH**" – when only the technical cues are rehearsed. During the tech, the actors work for the **STAGE CREW** (so the crew can rehearse their cues). There follows a **DRESS RUN**, when acting, costume, lights, sound and effects are all put together.

The Read-through

You should come to rehearsal with your script and a notebook, or your workbook (see page 84). If at all possible, you should have read the play through on your own before this rehearsal. Always take notes at this stage. You should take notes when you first read the play, and again at first reading with the company. First impressions are extremely important and fade quickly, so record them. Refer to them regularly throughout the rehearsal period. The director often talks a lot out of sheer nerves, and most of this talking is lost on the actors who are also too nervous to listen. Always take notes. When you read through as a company, it is your job to *communicate* the text. Look up at the person you are addressing (see Auditions on page 76) and remind yourself that this is an important first rehearsal.

After the read-through, a discussion may take place. This is often useful in setting the world of the play and the production (hopefully related). Don't feel you *have* to speak.

Research

Research is the way you discover the world of the play you are bringing to life, and it varies depending on the play. For example, when working on an Expressionist play it would be appropriate to research Expressionist painting. The style can be used directly by an actor as, for example, images for a character. All realistic plays should be researched for their specific historical period, but keep the work of the actor in mind. What would an ordinary person of the time know? Concentrate on the detail of social history and the history of ordinary things. In Shakespeare's time, for instance, a woman (with one or two notable exceptions) had a choice of being a wife, daughter, whore or nun. This strongly affects the choices they make or their strength of character in making certain choices. Pay attention to the culture surrounding the play when it was written, and your own culture. You should use libraries, museums, music, visual art, personal witnesses if they still exist, letters and documents of the period, and historical evidence to color and enrich your perception of the play.

A discussion is useful in order to understand the world of the play and the production.

Improvisations

These may not take place at all. You may discuss character and go straight to blocking. You may, however, have a problem you want to explore through improvisation, and this can be done with the director or on your own with fellow actors. It is vital to define the *purpose* of the improvisation. Are you exploring the action of the scene (page 79), the relationship or aspects of your character (page 84)?

You should also come to all rehearsals suitably dressed. Would you be prepared to roll around on the floor in the clothes you are wearing? If the answer is no, you're wearing the wrong clothes!

Choices

Within the factual framework of the play, your job as an actor is to make choices. Choice of action, activities, objectives and characteristics must all be explored in rehearsal. You make these choices in partnership with a director. Because the director is responsible for the total play and not just your bit of it, the director's decision must prevail and you must trust that decision, even if it does not seem to be the best for you. Your job is a paradox. You must make bold choices, believe in them, defend them in argument if appropriate but, at the same time, be flexible enough to modify or even discard them in the final interests of the play.

Blocking the Play

Blocking, or working out where you stand and your moves, is sometimes seen as an old-fashioned way of working. Actors who know what they are doing in a scene and are clear about their character's relationship to other characters should be able to find their way around the stage, creating an organic, spontaneous feel to the scene. Most directors, however, will have to block parts of the play – that is, they will tell you where to stand and when and how to move. Group scenes invariably need blocking so that the action can be seen. Make sure you know the terms used to instruct actors where to move on stage (page 75). The actor's job is to bring these mechanical instructions to life by *justifying* them. You must motivate the character so that the director's mechanical instruction is brought to life.

Learning Lines

Two factors determine when you must do this. The first is the style of the director and the second is the style of the play.

Some directors will do a read-through, talk about the play and characters, then expect you to have learned your lines before they rehearse any further with you. They might say, "You can't act with a book in your hand." You may find it difficult to learn lines like this because you will have to learn them by rote. You will not fully understand the intention behind the words. The worst pitfall with early line learning is that you learn the lines in blocks, without much attention to sense or communication, and then find you have learned some inappropriate stresses and rhythms that are very hard to unlearn and eradicate. For this reason, many directors encourage you not to learn lines until you are absolutely sure of their meaning. You should normally have worked through the scene thoroughly with the director. When the time comes to learn the lines, do so carefully, paying attention to the lines of thought and intention of your character. The lines should then come easily because they make logical sense.

When working on your own, without the director, it is tempting to use your time with your fellow actors for "line bashing." This means saying the lines over and over again. Try to avoid this, as you will lose expression. Play the scene, and the lines should then come naturally and in an integrated way.

Sometimes the style of the play will demand that the lines be learned before complex physical work can start. Farce is like this, while complex musical routines that incorporate dialogue demand formal line learning. In these cases it is best to have line rehearsals, where contact and intention can be established with players even as the lines are being "pressure-learned."

Line rehearsals are sometimes called late in the process, where the dialogue is spoken without reference to blocking (where you stand) or business (what you actually do, such as drinking a cup of tea). This enlivens the process and returns the actor to the actual text, from which he or she may have strayed during rehearsal.

Costume and Props

You will find that the process of rehearsal involves continuous incorporation of new material. Each time a new element appears in the production, a mechanistic atmosphere intrudes that seems to weigh down your previous confidence. Conventionally, props arrive during final runs, just before dress rehearsal. Conventionally, actors always break them! You will have been working with all "practical" props (those that actually function and which you have to use), or a practical substitute, since very early in rehearsal. Make it your business to secure substitute props and then you will not get a nasty shock just when the pressure on you is greatest.

Be pleasant to the stage crew and wardrobe staff. Don't make the arrogant mistake of regarding them as your creative inferiors. Take personal responsibility for checking that your personal props are all where they should be backstage. However large the stage staff, you should always do this for your own peace of mind.

The Rehearsal Pattern

This is a typical rehearsal pattern developing towards a performance, starting with auditions and finishing with press night.

Auditions. The director auditions the actors, who then form a company.

First rehearsal. The first rehearsal is usually a read-through of the play followed by a discussion, but may begin elsewhere – for example, with improvisation.

Discovering the world of the play. Early rehearsals in a long rehearsal period may include improvisation to discover the world of the play or the style of the text. This may include research and discussion.

Systematic rehearsal. Depending on the play, scenes may be rehearsed in a chronological or thematic order. This will involve analysis of text and discussion or improvisation from the analysis. Character may be explored through improvisation at this stage.

Blocking the play. If the rehearsal period is very short (weekly rep, for instance, means just that – one week), this might be all you see of the director!

Costume and props. Normally you will find substitute props, or if the prop is "practical" (you actually have to use it), you will be practicing now. Acrobatic and physical routines should be well advanced. Use appropriate pieces of your own clothing to give you a feel for the period.

Off the book. At this point, all lines should be learned, so you should no longer be holding the text of the play in your hand.

Rehearsal for contact and style. The focus of rehearsal is now to bring the scene to life.

The run-through. This is both for single acts and the whole play. At first apparently clumsy, the work of the rehearsal quickly begins to show itself and the actor gains a sense of his or her role in the whole work.

Technicalities now start to intervene and you sometimes feel as though you have to juggle props and costume as well as act. Apparently intractable technical problems and irritations quickly yield to a little technical rehearsal!

The technical rehearsal. This is exactly what it means. It is not concerned with the acting, nor is it for the actors except when they have a technical job to do. In a technical rehearsal, the stage crew rehearse all the technical cues, and the actors stand by in case they are needed. Actors rehearse the technical moments in the play which involve them, such as scene changes.

The "dress and tech." This is the stage where your acting combines with the technical elements of the production, which now only needs an audience. There will sometimes be a photocall.

The photocall. The play is photographed, starting at the end and finishing at the start of the play (Scene 1) so that the production is then ready to proceed.

Public dress rehearsal. There is sometimes a public dress rehearsal ("PDR"). The play is "run in" in front of an invited or informal audience. This may finish with a press night.

Press night. After this, you can only wait for the reviews!

Theatre Spaces

It should be remembered that producers of theatre, whether small or great, have used the widest imaginable range of environments to stage their shows, including disused municipal swimming pools, the street, warehouses and dockyard buildings, the upper rooms of bars and a defunct railroad terminus. Here are four examples of purpose-built theatres that create a specific actor/audience relationship.

Proscenium-arch Theatre

Nicola Sabbattini (1574–1654) invented the proscenium arch, or "picture frame," to hide the machinery that created the mechanical magic of theatre. Landscapes and seascapes could be created using the newly discovered technique of perspective, and animated by painted "flats" of canvas on wooden frames. These could be slid into the "wings" at the side of the frame, or into the "flies" above it to change the scene. In order to benefit fully from these magical illusions, it was necessary for the audience to sit facing the frame in parallel rows, and this relationship – an audience in front of a frame – is how most of us imagine a traditional theatre.

In the nineteenth century, when electric lighting was brought to these theatres, it became too expensive to light the auditorium, so only the stage was lighted. The actors, unable to see the audience, were unable to play directly to them and began instead to play to each other.

The proscenium-arch theatre lends itself pre-eminently to the theatre of the "fourth wall," that is, the audience eavesdrops on the stage action, which is felt to occur privately: behind the "fourth wall" that is framed by the proscenium arch.

The Portland Center for the Performing Arts, Oregon, USA.

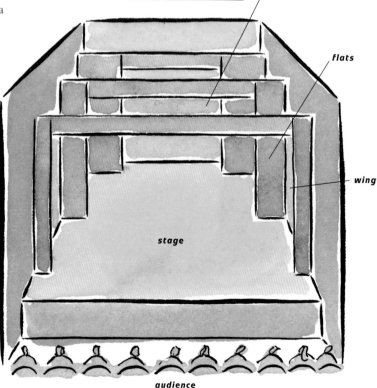

flies

flats

wing

stage

A proscenium-arch theatre.

audience

Theatre-in-the-round

The primary relationship between actors and their audience was probably the circle. Tribal dance dramas are invariably acted out in a circle. In classical Athens, the almost circular Theatre of Dionysius is evidence that the democratic nature of the state extended even to watching plays. In this theatre, made of stone with stone seating, you can hear a pin drop at any position in the auditorium. When the audience surrounds the dramatic action, there are no "best seats," and an intimacy comes from the fact that everybody feels close to the action.

Many modern theatres have returned to this basic relationship. At every position in the auditorium, the audience has a shifting experience of the action. The actor's back will often be facing the audience, but this doesn't matter if the space is intimate because it feels as though you are playing in a large room.

In larger theatres-in-the-round, the actor may be blocked to "play the diagonal" between the four entrance spaces so that the action can be clearly seen. This is not an arrangement that lends itself to stage illusion. There is usually no scenery, and props and furniture are minimal; scene changes are therefore problematic.

The New Victoria Theatre in Staffordshire, England. This is an example of a theatre-in-the-round.

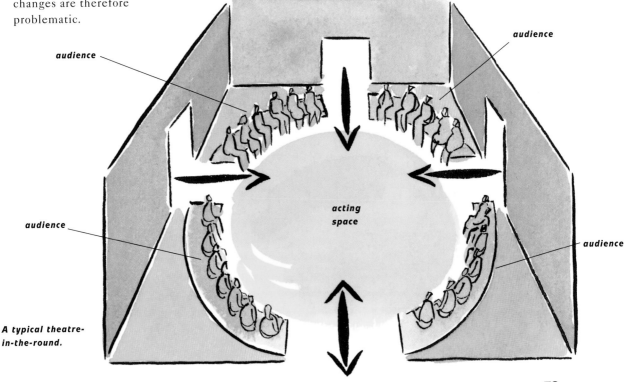

A typical theatre-in-the-round.

audience

audience

audience

audience

acting space

The Thrust Stage

The thrust stage combines the possibilities of illusion and intimacy. The audience sits around three sides of a stage which "thrusts" into the auditorium. The fourth side belongs to the actors. It may have entrance doors for the actors, as in Shakespeare's Globe Theatre, or it may have a proscenium arch cut into it, behind which sliding and flying scenery can change the setting. The Restoration Drury Lane theatre in London was like this. Many modern theatres combine a thrust stage with a proscenium arch, allowing the actor/audience relationship the flexibility to move from formal to intimate.

Promenade

The promenade or "walkabout" theatre space has dispensed altogether with the stage. The actors find their own playing space and the audience rearrange themselves to watch. This relationship has a long and honorable history, particularly in medieval theatre, where "stytlers," medieval bouncers, would push and shove the audience into position under the direction of the "ordinary," or stage manager/prompter, making space for the processions, songs, dances and dramatic scenes of the mystery and morality plays.

In modern theory, a form of mêlée was recommended by Antonin Artaud (1896–1948), the French theatre director. Street theatre and other unconventional venues employ this of necessity, but many conventional theatres that are able to remove their stages will also use it. The actor must draw out and focus the attention of the audience at the beginning of each scene or its concentration will gradually disperse. Promenade staging works best for plays that have a robust acting style and a mixture of song, dance and scene play.

A thrust stage, where the audience sits around the three sides of the stage.

*A performance of **The Good Woman of Setzuan** acted as a promenade at the Orange Tree Theatre in London.*

Moving around the Stage

There are certain conventions that actors and directors use when moving around the stage. A director might ask you to "walk down center" or to "enter from stage left and turn downstage. . .," and so on. Look at the picture below, which is a plan of a proscenium-arch stage (see page 72).

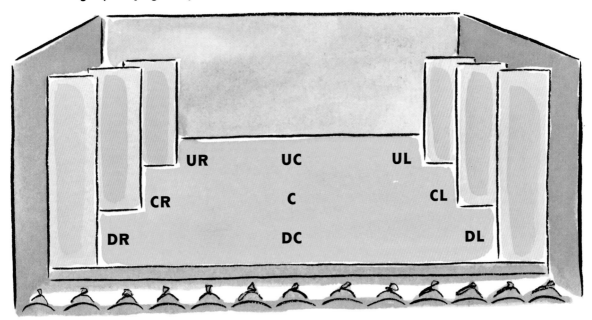

UR   **UC**   **UL**

CR   **C**   **CL**

DR   **DC**   **DL**

U = Upstage, which means away from the audience

D = Downstage, or toward the audience

L and R = toward the left or right as you look at the audience

C = Center stage

Face your partner at some distance, imagining that you are an actor on stage, and your partner is the audience. Let your partner read the following instructions, and you respond to them. If you have no partner, speak this on to a tape.

Exercise

Moving on Stage

1 Stand center stage.
2 Look into the wings, stage right, then left. . . .
3 Now look out (meaning "to the audience"). Give a knowing wink!
4 Move slowly down center. Stop on a thought. Run off up right.
5 Run on down right. Relief! Beckon to the wings up left. Put a hand in your pocket as though about to produce something. Look out. Search all your pockets. Run up center.
6 Turn down center. Look out. Shrug. Run off up left.

Auditions

Auditions are very important, so you should learn how to audition well and avoid the errors that are commonly made.

First Principles

👍 DO lots of auditions! Auditioning is a skill to be learned, so practice.

👍 DO keep a record of all auditions. Record the name of the company, note the company repertoire and style, the composition of the audition panel, the name and position of everyone you met and brief notes for reference next time you audition.

👎 DON'T take rejection personally. To do this is unprofessional self-indulgence. You may have been rejected for quite arbitrary reasons that have nothing to do with your talent or your chances of getting work. Regard all feedback as a gift. Take advice, try again, and remember that persistence is the most important personal quality for an actor.

👎 DON'T brood on your mistakes. Finish the audition and *forget it*.

Turn out slightly from the hip for a Restoration effect.

This posture (with your legs crossed) is unsuitable for female characters before 1920.

Preparation

👍 DO your research. If you have time, find out about the style and repertoire of the company.

👎 DON'T, for example, turn up to audition for a company which has a classical repertoire, dressed in dungarees, ready to do your clown show for under-fives!

👍 DO obtain and read the play if you can. Note down your first impressions.

👍 DO dress appropriately (but not literally) for the character. For instance, if the part is a whore, you don't dress like a whore, though you may use sexy clothes. Clean jeans and denim jacket might be appropriate for a cowhand – the director must be able to see the character in you. In general, don't grow a beard or put on heavy make-up. Let the director *see* you.

DO prepare appropriate classical and modern audition speeches if asked to do so. Classical means before 1900 and modern means after 1900. Select one of each. You should have several to choose from. They should be less than two minutes' duration (shorter is better than longer). Read the plays that contain the speeches in case the director wishes to discuss the context of the speech with you.

DO select or send an appropriate photograph. This means a photograph of you that looks like you.

DO check your résumé to make sure you feel easy about discussing everything on it. A résumé should be upbeat to get you to the interview, but don't include anything you can't justify.

DON'T pester the office of the company that has called the audition. Don't phone to ask unnecessary questions. If you are invited to inquire by phone, prepare your questions in advance, and write them down. Listen to the answers and take written notes.

DO note the date, place and time of the audition and take this with you.

Look at your lines. "Connect" with the speech, look up and communicate.

On the Day

DO leave yourself plenty of time and space. Avoid hangovers or over-tight schedules that will only add to the stress of the occasion. Prepare your clothes, notes, etc., the night before and have an early night.

DON'T be late! Walk into the building five minutes before your appointment.

DON'T get angry if they're running late, or for any reason. Take out your frustration in the gym or by jogging!

DO be nice to the secretary, cleaner, voluntary helper and assistant stage manager. They may well be asked later what they think of you!

DO compose yourself. Don't chatter to other people who are auditioning or do anything that will disturb your concentration.

DO be yourself. Don't try to be someone else, or compare yourself with them.

DO put yourself in the shoes of those who are auditioning you. If you are right for the job, they will have done their job perfectly and everyone can go home. They *want* you to be good.

When You Go in

👍 DO behave in a confident, relaxed way. If *you* think you're no good, so will they.

👍 DO take your time. Get the feel of the space. There will probably be a chair and table if you need it. Ask for what you want. Arrange the furniture if necessary before you start.

👍 DO direct your piece out front so that the panel can see clearly what you are doing.

👎 DON'T use the audition panel as characters in the scene. This is off-putting to directors, who need to take notes. Directors also need a sense of distance.

👎 DON'T ever apologize, whatever happens. Never ask for sympathy, verbally or with body language.

When using chairs as "other characters", don't choose a scene that is full of people.

This is the correct position.

Here, the position with the chair is incorrect.

Your nerves and self-doubts are of no interest to the casting panel!

👍 DO *listen* to advice, instruction or communication offered to you by the panel. Even if you are nervous, you must come across as *responsive* and *receptive*.

👍 DO center and compose yourself before you start.

👎 DON'T ostentatiously "prepare." Most directors will simply think you are showing off and/or have a problem.

👍 DO your best, and finish in silence. The director will probably say thank you. Don't bow or say, "That's it!"

👎 DON'T ask unnecessary questions or try to chat with the panel.

👎 DON'T be upset or put off if the director works with you on your piece. It is a compliment, not a criticism! The director is trying to find out if you can respond to instructions and change what you do. Hear what is said to you and act boldly to do what is asked of you.

The Interview

👍 DO mentally prepare for this. Select a few topics from your résumé that are relevant and that interest you. You will undoubtedly be asked to "say something about yourself." Be factual and clear.

👎 DON'T criticize past employers, companies, conditions or directors.

👍 DO put the interviewer at ease. You must give them enough simple information to be able to ask you further questions. If you feel at ease, so will they.

👍 DO make the interviewer feel safe in your hands, and that you are not a risky proposition.

👎 DON'T diminish or play down what you have done, even if this is an interview for your first job.

👎 DON'T exaggerate or lie out of insecurity – you will simply look immature.

👍 DO remember that your brightness, enthusiasm and positive energy will help a director – to whom you are a stranger – take the risk of employing you.

Adjust your posture to give a period or "class" effect.

Don't "collapse" into a mistake – make it work!

Sight-reading

👎 DON'T be thrown if the director gives you a piece of text and asks you to read cold. Ask for a couple of minutes to look at the passage.

👍 DO *communicate* the text to the panel. This is much more important than getting it accurate.

👍 DO *look up*. Don't bury your head in the text. Let the director see you.

👎 DON'T stop and start again if the text takes an unexpected turn. *Accommodate* the unexpected.

Let the director see you.

Don't rush. Silence is interesting.

Communication is more important than accuracy.

Afterwards

👍 DO retain your sense of humor!

👍 DO forgive yourself immediately for any mistakes.

👍 DO enjoy the prospect of the next audition!

Preparing the Text

A theatre production is an act of imaginative collaboration between different sorts of artists. During the rehearsal period, the actor makes artistic choices in collaboration with fellow actors and the director.

These choices fall into two categories. The actor's first job is to analyze the text and turn the dialogue into psychological and physical "things to do." Unless an actor knows what to do (as opposed to what to say), he or she is lost. Second, the actor must gather from the text evidence of the qualities, physical and psychological, of the character to be portrayed. This evidence must also be turned into "things to do," or it will remain useless.

Text preparation may well take place in rehearsal, many choices being made in discussion with the director. Some directors are teaching directors but many are not, and will simply explain what they expect of you, without indicating how you might achieve what they want.

Text analysis can, if necessary, be done alone and can help you in the following ways. First, it helps you to be specific, to choose the *exact* word to describe your motivation, and it helps you apply yourself to the text moment to moment. Second, it provides you with an approach to problems, when it seems that nothing is happening and you don't know why. Third, it is the basis for improvising around the text.

Some Principles of Text Analysis

Analyzing the text helps you to understand how to play your particular character and to understand the play as a whole.

Action

Acting is *action*. Nobody speaks to another person purely to hear the sound of his or her own voice. This is true in plays as in life. When characters in plays say something, they do so because they *want* something. The words spoken in the text are a clue to the "want," and the want is known as an action.

An action happens inside you; it is an *intention*. Consider a golf player about to make a putt, or a sprinter at the starting block. Neither person is physically doing anything, yet the observer is drawn irresistibly to them. Their psychological focus is so sharp that they clearly communicate their intention to us, and this intention does not stop when they start to move. On stage a similar heightened state of intention, underpinning the physical activity, makes the actor irresistibly watchable.

Improvisation 1

At the moment, you are reading this book. Invent a phrase that describes your action at this moment. To solve a problem? To rest and recover? To realize your ambitions? To improve yourself culturally? Continue to read, experimenting with a *want*, which you invent as *motivation* for reading this book. Be aware of how your focus on attention sharpens as you become conscious of the want, and how your energy changes as you change the want.

Exercise

Improvisation 2

Walk around the room. Stand still. Sit down. *Justify* everything you do. For example, walk around the room to check that nothing has been stolen, walk to pass the time, walk to calm your nerves. Stand still to listen. Stand still to think. Sit down to plan your day. Sit down because you're exhausted. Note the focus and change in your energy as the want changes.

Activities

The action, or want, is the inner life of the *activity*. If the action is *what* you want, then the activity is *how* you get it. Activities are about *tactics* and therefore involve the actor physically. Experience of life tells us that simply to want something does not solve our problems. There are all sorts of obstacles, inside us, in the world and in other people which either force us to struggle to achieve our ends, or to modify our desires in the face of adverse circumstances. This struggle forces us to change tactics continually. In a play, which is similar to life but heightened, focused and compressed, these changes of tactic (activities) create variety in the performance.

Exercise

Actions, Activities and Obstacles

1 Suppose I meet you to discuss a business deal and I try to get you to lend me some money (my action: to take money from you). You refuse point-blank (your action: to hold on to your money). This counteraction in the scene creates conflict.

2 I might change my action at this point and try to make friends in order to enlist your help in my business deal (my action: to bind with

you). On the other hand, I might continue to play my first action by using a succession of tactics (activities).

3 I might bully you.

4 I might try to make you feel like a cheapskate.

5 I might plead with you.

6 As a last resort, I might attack you. These are all activities, some physical, some psychological. If, when I attack you, you strike me down in self-defense, both of our actions have (in this case) resulted in a physical incident.

7 If I pretend to be more hurt than I really am (still playing my action), you might feel guilty and weaken (your feeling of guilt is an inner obstacle to achieving your want).

8 You might then change *your* action.

9 You are now seeking to get the best possible terms for your loan (your new action: to make a deal).

If all this took place in a play, we might generalize the scene as a heated argument. Such a generalization would not help the actor, who still would not know specifically what to do, apart from

⑥

⑦

Exercise

Inventing Actions

This is an exploration, not a performance. Recreate the elements of a space you find comfortable, such as your own room. Invent an action for yourself, perhaps to make your date fall in love with you, for example. Invent three physical activities (strategies) to do this. You might dress in some special clothes, arrange your hair with special care,

pay attention to the lighting, or perfume the room. The activities are ordinary and physical. Your action is your focus of concentration throughout the improvisation exercise. Practice this improvisation alone (your date never arrives!).

You could re-create an actual incident from your life. It can be special, but should not be traumatic – this would interfere with your exploration of the situation. If your fellow actors will watch you, so much the better. See if you can maintain concentration in public solitude – your concentration unaffected by their presence. Ask for their comments on your concentration.

get angry. By putting action into the text, you understand how to motivate the scene moment by moment. Inventing actions is part of the actor's creative input into the story.

Naturally, actions and activities must be drawn from the text and not pulled out of thin air – as an actor, you exist to serve the play. Although your choices of action will be limited and prescribed by the play, your choice of activities is much wider. (Notice, the verbs I used in the example for the actions: to take, to hold on to, to bind. They are all strong and active.)

⑧

⑨

Exercise

Power Play

Invent an action to play upon your partner. You wish them to do something simple for you, such as giving you a hug when leaving the room. This "want" must not be mentioned until you are certain your partner will do what you want, but it must be clearly phrased in your head. Employ different tactics (activities) to get what you want. Your partner should play along with the improvisation, accepting the situation, and creating obstacles but without making your task impossible.

The Given Circumstances and the Magic "If"

The given circumstances include everything you need to take into account when creating your role. This includes the plot of a play, its historical time, the setting of the action, its time of day, the season of the year, the interpretation of the actor and the director, scenery, props and lights. It is the living environment of the play, combined with the style of the production, that will condition your choices when deciding on actions and making character choices. Your preparation work must therefore include research, in order to clarify in your own mind the physical and social environment of the play. Character is formed, at least in part, by physical environment.

The "if" carries you into the imaginary circumstances of your character. Ask, "What would I do if I were . . . ?" By asking this question, you place yourself in the same position as your character and experience for yourself your character's problems in the play.

Imagine the character you are creating.

Exercise

"What If?"

While dressing yourself in the morning, apply the question, "What if?" Using the clothes you would ordinarily wear, put on your clothes as "if" you were preparing for the most important interview of your life. Or dress as "if" you were about to be executed. Or dress as "if" you had an important dinner date.

In each case, think specifically about the "given circumstances" surrounding your activity. Create from your imagination a world of circumstances around the activity.

Making a Workbook

The concepts and exercises I have described are not only applicable to everyday speech and activity, but can also be applied directly to dramatic texts, which are invariably heightened and compressed renderings of observable experience. This analysis is compiled in the actor's workbook.

A workbook is a script that you have fully annotated for your role in the play. You should prepare a blank workbook for the read-through and it will become a document of the tasks you must achieve, as well as a record of the rehearsal process.

First, photocopy the entire script. Buy a strong notebook, small enough to be held in one hand while rehearsing, but big enough to leave a broad margin around each photocopied page of script, and with more pages than the script.

Trim each page of script and stick it in the notebook. You will have a blank page opposite each page of text, and a broad margin around the text for notes. In the back of the book, there are blank pages for notes on the director's introduction, the style of the play, the style of production, general notes and commentary on character from text notes.

Highlight your lines (in yellow, for example) and mark the stage directions in another color. Write your action at the top of the scene and mark the text where the activities change. Mark any change or modification of action.

Note the circumstances of the scene (the circumstances of the play are noted in the back of the book). Note the magic "if" to remind you of the imaginative transformation.

A Sample Marked Script

The following example is the first scene of *Spring Awakening* by Frank Wedekind (1864–1918). Wendla is being fitted for her "woman's dress" by her mother, Frau Bergmann, on her fourteenth birthday. The script is marked by the actress playing Wendla.

It is marked in pencil, so that the notes can be changed according to the director's decisions, and according to the dynamic tension between herself and the actress playing Frau Bergmann. They are to be discussed, tried out, adapted and changed if necessary.

Spring Awakening: Wendla

MY ACTION
Change mother's mind on the grown-up dress

CIRCUMSTANCES
The time: 1892
The place: Germany
It is my 14th birthday
I am alone with mother
Mother is fitting me for my grown-up dress

The action takes place in a provincial town in Germany, 1891-1892.

(Activities)
To blame

MY OBJECTIVE
To remain a little girl

Living room.
WENDLA. (A) Why have you made my dress so long, mother?
FRAU BERGMANN. You're fourteen today.
WENDLA. I'd rather not have been fourteen if I'd known you'd make my dress so long.
FRAU BERGMANN. Your dress isn't too long, Wendla. What next? Can I help it if my child is four inches taller every spring? A grown girl can't still go round dressed like a little princess.

To plead with

WENDLA. At least the little princess's dress suits me better than this nightshirt. (B) Let me wear it once more, mother. One more long summer. Fourteen or fifteen, that's still soon enough for this sackcloth, Let's keep it till my next birthday. I'd only trip over the braid and tear it.
FRAU BERGMANN. I don't know what I should say. I'd willingly keep you exactly as you are, darling. Other girls are stringy or plump at your age. You're not. Who knows what you'll be like when they're grown up?

To threaten

WENDLA. (C) Who knows – perhaps I won't be anything anymore.
FRAU BERGMANN. Child, child, where d'you get these ideas?

To protect

WENDLA. (D) Don't mummy. Don't be sad.
FRAU BERGMANN (*kisses her*). My precious.

To embarrass

WENDLA. They come to me in the evening when I can't sleep. And it doesn't make me the least bit sad, and I go to sleep better then. (E) Is it a sin to think about such things, mother?
FRAU BERGMANN. Go and hang the sackcloth in the wardrobe. Put your little princess's dress on again and God bless you. When I get a moment I'll sew a broad flounce round the bottom.

Yes! Action achieved. Joy! Energy!

WENDLA (*hanging the dress in the wardrobe*). No, I'd rather even be twenty than that …!

"If" I were 14 today.
"If" mother and I only had each other.
"If" I were changing into a woman.

Preparing the Role

***Character transformation is one of the great delights of acting.
To reveal yourself through the life of another (stage) person is a
challenge and a responsibility.***

You can only use yourself, your body, your
feelings and your experience. You must do
this in a way which serves the character and,
through the character, the play. You must "yield"
to the character.

Points to Remember

● The script comes first! Characterization involves a multitude of choices,
but don't make any until you have thoroughly researched the script. It is
the script that limits what you can do.

In your workbook, make three columns on a blank page at the back. Then
read through the text and note the columns:

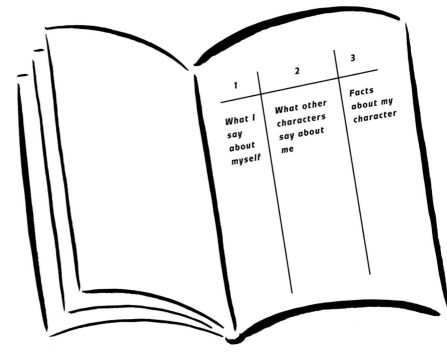

1 What the character says
about him/herself (what I
say about myself).

2 What other characters say
about my character (what
others say about me).

3 Facts. For example, this is
a woman; she has had five
children. (Beware of
making value judgements.
You should stick to the
facts only.)

1	2	3
What I say about myself	What other characters say about me	Facts about my character

Judge for yourself whether your character or others in the play talk honestly about themselves and others, and make a note of your opinions. You will have discovered a great deal even if your character says nothing about himself or herself. You will have discovered the extent of your freedom to invent. Come to the character "innocent," that is, try to have no preconceptions at all.

● Transform *yourself*, not the character! Avoid the temptation to make the character more like you. For example, people who don't like playing old characters might be tempted to make a 60-year-old character, say, 50. Or to make character choices that are more likeable or sympathetic. This is not allowed. It makes for very boring work. Decide early in the process how old the character is.

● *Empathic* characterization. You do not personally have to like your character. You may not approve of the way they behave; you may find their morals disgusting. Your opinions are of absolutely no consequence and must be set aside. Suspend your judgement and awaken your curiosity. You must be able to develop an emphatic relationship with your character, stand in their shoes emotionally, and see the world from their point of view. Only in this way will you be able to yield to the character and fully create him or her, undistorted by your own judgements.

Casual or rigid? Relaxed or awkward?

Impulsive or smooth way of walking?

A Checklist of Characteristics

Put this checklist in the back of your workbook. As you go through the list, other qualities and characteristics may occur to you which you should *note down immediately*. However, do not rely too heavily on lists, and do not indulge in useless speculation. It is not necessary to know what your character did at the age of five unless the text implies that this is important. Lists of characteristics are only of use if you can find a way, psychologically or physically, of embodying them.

● **Age.** How old is the character exactly? How does the character show age? Is it important how they feel about their age? (A young girl may try to appear older, an older woman look like "mutton dressed as lamb".)

● **Sex.** Do they affirm or deny their male or their female sexuality? Do they exploit their sexuality? Do they use their sex to seduce or frighten others? Are they sexually "needy"? How is this expressed?

● **Height, weight, eye and skin type and color.** Is this character a small personality in a big body? A slim person in a fat body? Or does the personality match the physical body? Does this person feel/wish they were ugly/handsome? How do other characters relate physically to your character?

● **Physical style.** This is the carriage/posture of the character. Is he or she physically casual, relaxed, precise, rigid, awkward?

● **Body type.** Is the character an athletic type? Is he or she of heavy, medium or light build? What is the character's shape image: like a stalk, like an egg or like a lump of clay?

● **Movement.** What is the character's rhythm and way of walking – like a cat, for example, or quick, impulsive, smooth, jerky?

● **Voice and speech.** What is the most striking feature of the character's voice? Higher or lower pitch? Smooth or rough? Guttural? Stuttering? Eloquent? Clipped?

● **Appearance.** Does the character look attractive, clean, neat, fastidious, dirty, unkempt?

Return to this list throughout rehearsal, and revise it within the parameters of your script analysis as your impressions of your character become sharper.

Inner and Outer Characteristics

Answer the question: "Who am I?" as fully as you can. You must decide on the character's background, his or her likes and dislikes, relationships and characteristics.

Make a provisional list in your workbook of characteristics, using two columns headed "Inner Characteristics" and "Outer Characteristics." Inner and outer characteristics are not always the same. Outer characteristics embody the face that the character shows to the world, but the inner characteristics contain the actual inside world of the character that may sometimes surface, for example, when the character is alone. A character who shows a resolutely happy, bubbly exterior may be hiding an inner sadness. The character may feel generous on the inside, but this may express itself to others as extravagance. On the other hand, a character may be gentle, loyal or weak, through and through, inside and out.

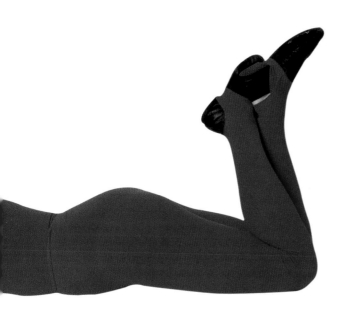

Imagery

When you apply imagery, you move from a thinking to a feeling, and an instinctive response to the character. Apply the following questions, remembering that the answers can't be wrong, nor can they be logically argued. Try to let the answer float into your mind before you examine it!

- If my character were an animal, what sort of animal?

- If my character were an hour of the day, what hour?

- If my character were the weather, what sort of weather?

- If my character were a landscape, what sort of landscape?

- If my character were a season of the year, what season?

- If my character were an element (earth, air, fire, water), which element?

And so on. If the answers to these questions make you want to try out something physically, don't hesitate!

The Physical Transformation into Character

By now you should have enough information to begin to transform yourself physically into your character. This whole process holds good for *all* characters, including non-speaking parts. The less said about the character in the text, the more freedom you have to invent.

The raised center

The Shifting Center

Imagine that your limbs do not move as the result of your decision, but that you *are* moved by a power center in the middle of your chest (this is not a physical or vocal center, it is an imagined center). Let this center in the middle of your chest power your limbs. Make some simple movements. Walk, stand, sit down, powered by the center.

When you have the sensation of moving from the center, and are confident that you can let it "power" you with different speeds and qualities of energy, try moving the center into different parts of your body.

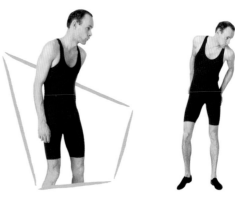

The lowered center

The center in the eye

It is very important that you remain conscious of how these shifting centers make you feel. Each sensation begins a journey. As you respond to the sensation, the physical awareness develops and strengthens.

Now apply this exercise to your character. Do you raise or lower the center as you transform yourself into the character? Characterize the center that moves your character . . . . Is it wet or dry? Hot or cold? Is it small, like a pin or a marble? Or large like a big, wet, warm towel? How does the energy from the center power your body? Does it flow, seep, gush, pulse or stream?

The center just off the tip of the nose

Marianne is working on The Mother by Stanislau Ignacy Witkiewicz (1885–1939). She is working on the title character, using the images of "demanding of" and "collapsing in the presence of." She makes the first gesture, allowing its weight, timing and character to develop, then she constructs the "collapsing," and finally puts both together in a single gesture.

The Psychological Gesture

Choose from your list of characteristics one that makes you want to move. Characteristics like "restless," "overbearing" or "grasping" are dynamic and are therefore better than characteristics like "kind" or "loyal." You are going to make the characteristic physical by turning it into a gesture.

First move your body and limbs to give the characteristic a shape. This is not a generalized cliché, but a shape that expresses this characteristic in your character. *Do* it rather than think it through. The shape will have a beginning, a middle and an end. It is a deliberate gesture. Refine the shape. Work on it as a sculptor works on a shape. This shape, however, is dynamic. It has weight, rhythm and speed. Work at it until it feels correct.

Then choose another, different characteristic. It might be a contrasting inner and outer characteristic (for example, idealistic as an inner characteristic, escapist as an outer characteristic). Develop this contrasting gesture. Finally, incorporate the two, making the change thoroughly physical. Enjoy the contrast and the change, and enjoy the characterization in your body.

Tim is doing Nightingale from Vieux Carré by Tennessee Williams (1911–1983). He is working on being "needy" and "withdrawn," constructing both impulses in detail and then combining them. This is an expressionistic exercise.

Animals

Think of an animal that has some qualities in common with your character. Is it possible for you to make this animal, and create these qualities in the animal? Choose a mammal rather than a fish, or an insect. Begin to work on *totally* transforming into the animal.

Find the means to observe your chosen animal. You can go to a zoo or a farm, or you can use videos or both, but you need to be able to observe the animal in its natural physical state – using its normal energy when not stressed or frightened. Ask yourself the following questions about the animal. What is the *furthest* imaginative distance you must travel to create the animal – in other words, what is it about the animal that is least like you? Do not make your decisions before you make your observations, or you will get a dead cliché instead of a live animal.

Questions to Ask Yourself

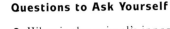

● What is the animal's inner and outer tempo (the quickness or slowness of movement, inside and outside)? The animal might have a quick inner tempo and a slow outer tempo, the reverse of this, or a totally slow or totally quick tempo.

● Examine the animal's use of its senses. What is the animal's primary sense? Sight? Smell? Hearing? How do you know?

● What shapes does the animal make? Is it a horizontal or vertical animal? Imagine or draw physical shapes made by this animal, using a single line.

● Is it a carnivore or herbivore? What is its jaw action?

● What is its lung capacity? How do you know?

● How does it move and act?

● How does it eat?

● How does it carry its weight?

● Where is its center of gravity?

● Choose a word to describe the animal's inner life.

Padding can be used once the weight and center of gravity of the animal has been established.

Marianne is creating a stork, which will develop into a hysterical woman.

Chloe is using elements of a camel to find character qualities.

Now work on making these answers a physical reality. Wear a leotard. The less you wear, the more you have to use your body to transform.

When you have begun to find the elements of your transformation, you may consider using padding if appropriate. Create a small scenario in which the animal changes, revealing something new about its nature. For example, a stag at bay is a different animal from a stag grazing. Practice this scenario as an exercise.

When you are absolutely physically confident with your animal, use it to establish the physical qualities of your character. You do not necessarily need the whole animal. Features and "essences" can be used. You can use the animal to enrich the inner life of your character. You will already have made some bold, colourful choices in building your character.

Combining animal qualities with costume conjures up the physically transformed character.

Costumes and Props

Some costumes and props transform you when you use them. They can be used to "hook in" to the character. Some actors have to find the shoes of their character before they can finish their work. Props and costume elements are sensory aids to character. Consider changes in hairstyle. Hair is one of the major sensory cues into character. These things make you *feel* different, so they can be useful in the middle stages of rehearsal, off the book, when you want to feel like the character, not yourself.

In rehearsal, using bits of substitute costume can help you find the style of the piece. A collar that holds you at the neck and a cummerbund or tied strip of cloth to hold you at the waist will help you to be more formal and less modern in your movements, early in rehearsal. Heeled boots and "character shoes" also give a more formal feel, as does the practice skirt.

Hats, like shoes, are full of character, and can quickly convey a strong period feel. They can give a feeling both for character and style, as can a stick.

A prop often has meaning which goes beyond its everyday use. Props that involve activity or labor, such as knitting, spinning and digging, involve rhythms which are part of the overall rhythm of the scene. Sometimes the rhythm of the activity reflects how the character feels inside. Fear, anger, faraway thoughts and stubborness all affect the use of the working prop which, if used skilfully, can express the inner life of a character. Bertolt Brecht (1898–1956) made particular use of this and wrote it into the action of his scripts. Obviously, such props must be found and used very early in the rehearsal.

Basic Make-up

Under stage lights, your skin will look pale and facial features will be difficult to see from where the audience sits. Stage make-up defines your features and helps you create your character.

When preparing for make-up, use a toning lotion or astringent (according to your skin type) before applying foundation. To keep your skin in good condition you must, of course, remove your make-up properly after every performance. Avoid soap and water; use a good cleansing cream or lotion.

Foundation is the basis of stage make-up. Always use it, unless you have a skin that is dark and even in tone, have a good suntan, or need to look tired or sick. If you are dark-skinned or tanned and need foundation, match the color to your own skin. Women should choose a color darker than their own skin and men need a couple of shades darker than that, or the skin will look soft and feminine. If you are darker-skinned, don't attempt to look paler, or you will in fact look gray. Redheads and other fair-skinned people may find that foundation looks orange on them – if so, use a color a couple of shades lighter than the recommended shade.

Foundations are available in fluid, cream and cake form. Fluid foundations sometimes give inadequate cover for the stage. Cream foundations are widely used for the theatre and are ideal for women, but not those with greasy skins. Cake foundations are ideal for men and children, and also make the best body make-up.

Materials and Equipment

toner and cleanser	cake foundation
cream eye shadow	cream foundation
powder eye shadow	hair color
eyeliner	hair gel
eyebrow pencil	ready-made
mascara	beard/moustache
lip liner	natural sponge
lipstick	crêpe hair
highlight	latex
shader	spirit gum remover
rouge	spirit gum
powder	collodion
fluid foundation	

Foundation is the basis for make-up.

Use the palest, but not white, professional loose translucent powder.

Keep some good-quality brushes in a selection of shapes and sizes for different uses.

Use a toning lotion or astringent before applying foundation. Unperfumed baby wipes make good cleansers for children.

Have a plentiful supply of tissue and absorbent cotton.

You should have powder, cream and grease shaders in various darkish tones. Highlight with cream or grease in lighter shades.

You need powder and cream eye shadows in assorted colors.

Assorted colors of block and brush mascaras, together with pencil, cake and liquid eyeliner are needed.

Use rouge powder for general work, but have some cream rouge (liner) for special uses.

Aquacolors come in palettes like watercolor paints; rinse brushes in water.

Keep a selection of lipstick colors, including natural shades, matching lip liners, and gloss.

Keep an assortment of natural and synthetic sponges, and a velour puff for powdering. Sponge hair curlers are also useful.

Dressed wigs and ready-made moustaches and beards can be rented. Crêpe hair or wool comes in long plaits. Trim false eyelashes to fit if necessary. You should also remember bobby pins and hairnet, as well as colored hairsprays, gels, brushes and combs.

The main items used for special effects are: rigid collodion; wax; Leukoflex; spirit gum; latex; "blood."

Make-up for Women

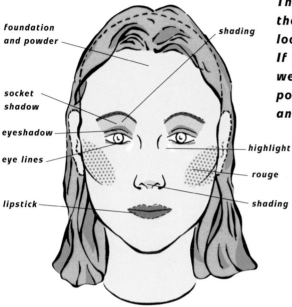

foundation
and powder

shading

socket
shadow

eyeshadow

eye lines

highlight

rouge

lipstick

shading

This make-up is suitable for small theatres where the audience is close. It looks attractive but definitely made-up. If you want to look as if you are not wearing make-up, change the rouge position, use highlight as eye shadow and choose a natural color for the lips.

③

②

①

1 Apply a little fluid or fine-textured foundation evenly with a sponge. Using a little shader on a brush, put a stroke of color under the eyebrows on the browbone, and another across the end of the nose from nostril to nostril.

2 The shading on the browbone increases the emphasis of the eyes. Blend the shading over the whole bone area. When the make-up is finished, this balancing shadow seems to disappear, but in fact it makes a big difference to the apparent size of the eyes. Blend the nose shading, curving up slightly over the tip.

3 Large eyelids make the eyes appear larger. Use pale neutral colors like this gray-green. Dark, smudgy eye shadow makes most eyes look smaller. On black and darker skin tones, bronzes and lilacs are attractive. Take the eye shadow over the entire eyelid. Powder shadow should be applied later, after powdering.

4 Powder the face. Don't forget the eyelids, because cream eye shadow will line without it and powder shadow will be difficult to blend evenly. Take a fine line of powder shadow along the roots of the lower eyelashes under the eyes, using dark brown, except with black hair. Don't go right up to the corners; straighten out when you reach that point, but don't extend the line.

5 A socket shadow gives extra definition. Use the same color as under the eyes but apply it with a larger brush. Lift the eyebrows and feel for the edge of the eye socket, brushing the shadow along it in a soft curve to give a mist of color, not a hard line. If you can't see it when you look in the mirror, it is too low and has disappeared into the crease of the lid.

6 Apply rouge over the cheek-bones and in the hollows underneath to emphasize the cheekbones and add warmth. White skins need a peachy tone; olive skins should have a deeper, more rusty shade, while black skins need a rich, dark color. Be careful with anything that has a blue tone, as it can change under the lights and gels. If the rouge streaks, the foundation hasn't been powdered properly.

7 Finally, you should apply lipstick with a brush, filling in the whole shape and working from the outer corners toward the center of the mouth. You can outline the lips with lip liner, but make sure it doesn't show when you have finished. The color depends on whether you want the mouth to look made-up or not, but avoid brown- or blue-toned lipsticks. These don't work well under lights.

Make-up for Men

This make-up is suitable for small theatres where you need as little as possible. You do need some make-up, because lighting drains the skin color, but all you need is foundation. The make-up on the black actor adds definition to the face.

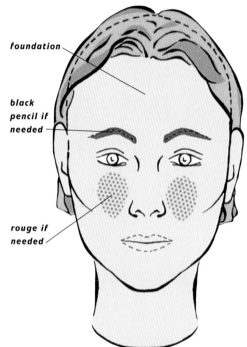

foundation

black pencil if needed

rouge if needed

1 This is how the actor looks naturally and, even after being made-up, the aim is for a natural look. Do not use too much; you can always add more make-up later if necessary.

2 Pat skin tonic over the whole face with cotton balls to remove any stickiness from the skin; it makes cake make-up difficult to apply evenly.

3 Stroke foundation on all the large areas of the face before you begin to blend. If you work on one section at a time, you will end up with a patchy look. Don't forget to cover the ears, neck and hands.

*foundation
and powder*

*black
pencil*

1 If the actor's skin is in good
condition with even color, you
won't need a foundation.
Otherwise, choose a color to
match the skin, using either a
cream base or a thin cake make-
up. Apply it over the whole face
and blend it under the chin.
Apply a cream highlight to the
eyelids. Dab highlights on each
lid and blend over the whole
eyelid.

2 Powder the whole face with
loose translucent powder,
remembering the eyelids. The
powder will reduce the shine on
the skin but leave a slight
sheen. If you use cake
foundation, you will only need
to powder the eyelids.

3 Brush through the eyebrows,
and add a little black pencil or
cake mascara to strengthen the
shape if they need more color.
Draw a fine line of black along
the edge of the lower eyelid to
define the lower lid.

Chapter 4

The *Actor* in *Performance*

Bringing the Play to Life

As rehearsals near completion, the process of giving the text emotional and physical shape gives way to the task of bringing it to life.

In the early stages of rehearsal the actors are working with the director to bring acting solutions to problems they define together. This is very specific, careful work – the work of preparation for performance. There is, however, a point in the rehearsal process where this craftsmanlike approach must yield to spontaneity. After all, the audience is not interested in how hard you have worked or how difficult your part is, nor even that you had a bad cold halfway through rehearsal. The audience comes to see the ease and joy with which you bring the text to life. Of course, if you haven't worked thoroughly and specifically you will fall to pieces, but if you've done the work, trust it.

You are no longer in the moment.

You want to laugh.

The harder you try not to . . .

. . . the worse it gets! This is known as "corpsing" and is a sign that you need to get back into your role.

The Final Stages of Rehearsal

"There isn't enough money, and not enough time. The facilities are inadequate, the cast are far from perfect and not quite right for the play . . . . Rehearsals could have been organized better, or differently . . . ." If you are saying all or some of these things by the final stages of rehearsal, then you are in the company of all actors and all productions. The success or failure of a play rarely depends on any of these factors. Say these things to yourself if you must. Forget them, and get going with your job!

Refreshing Rehearsals and Keeping the Performance Fresh

At this stage, rehearsals can easily suffer from the problem of woodenness. Lines are always said in the same way, and moves can look automatic and dead. From the actor's point of view, everyone gets exactly what they expect. Deep inside, the actor goes into "automatic pilot," the director falls asleep or watches the rehearsal while mentally plotting the lights. At this stage it is useful to reintroduce the unexpected and let you, the actor, play the scene using your instincts rather than your habits. The following suggestions require you to play the scene using a *focus of concentration*. You must let the scene live moment by moment, at the same time playing the agreed game. The following exercises are also useful for refreshing long performance runs.

101

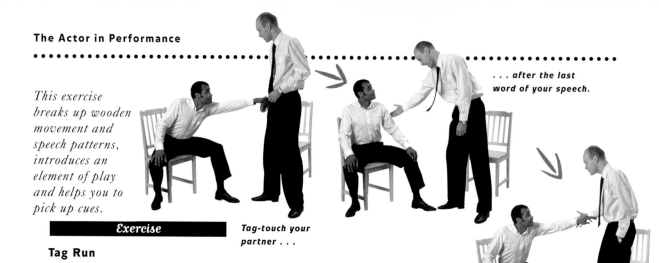

Tag-touch your partner . . .

. . . after the last word of your speech.

Speeches flow from one to the next.

Don't express tension.

This exercise breaks up wooden movement and speech patterns, introduces an element of play and helps you to pick up cues.

Tag Run

Tag-touch the next speaker at the end of your speech.
Sometimes the speaker will touch before the end of the speech. The next speech, beginning on the touch, introduces overlapping and simultaneous speaking. Players should work to release physical tension as they perform the exercise.

The following exercise creates physical intimacy and raises the emotional intensity of the scene through physical contact. It also breaks up speech and movement patterns.

Contact Run

Players may not say their lines unless they are touching the person to whom they are speaking. An observer must not see the touch as mechanical; it must look perfectly natural within the scene. Players must touch in a different way for each new thought. It is not sufficient to "hang on" to the person to whom you are speaking.

A player will often not be positioned correctly to touch the person he or she is speaking to. The player must fill the pause, integrate it into the scene, find a natural way to move into position, touch naturally and integrate all of these elements while continuing to play the scene.

Make sure you know what you're doing with the character in the scene before you do these exercises. You will no doubt go back to the agreed blocking and inflexions, but you will have experienced the scene from different angles. You will get nothing from these exercises unless you are prepared to respond in a new way to the unexpected. Hear the text as though it is for the first time and speak it as though you have never said it before.

Here are four "runs" that help with expression.

Exercise

Four Expressive Runs

1 Baby run. Play the scene as though you were two years old. This "permits" uninhibited physical and emotional expression.

2 Italian run. Play the scene like a cartoon Italian. This is especially good for inhibited actors! It's good for picking up cues, for emotional expressiveness and for showing the emotional changes.

3 Melodrama run. This is like a Victorian melodrama where all the "beats" are made physical. Well-chosen music is useful as a background, and accomplished players can try silent movie runs where all the dialogue is specifically made physical, so that an observer would be able to understand it word by word.

4 Sheet of glass. Actors behave as though a sheet of glass had been placed across the fourth wall, between stage and audience. The actors must convey all of the text through lip action and gesture, but without sound.

The Role of the Audience

It is the presence of a live audience before live actors that makes theatre different from television and film. The latter are more akin to sculpture, where the material (the performance) is cut into shape by an editor's knife and can be endlessly repeated. Each theatre performance, however, is unique and unrepeatable, relying as it does upon the live "electricity" between actor and audience. There can be no theatre without an audience, and in this sense all rehearsals are a guess – the production is an unknown quantity until the final piece of the jigsaw, the audience, is in place.

The audience is not passive; it participates actively in the event, as a group of individuals and as a unit. In some productions the audience sits in the dark with powerful lights blinding the actor to the sight of the audience. Yet, even in this atmosphere, which appears so alien to communication, the electricity between the actor and audience is almost palpable.

Audiences invariably enter a theatre with a feeling of enthusiastic expectation. They are almost never hostile to the actors or to the play. Even a controversial play will generate excited interest.

The relationship of the actor with the audience supplies the "electricity" that brings the performance to life.

Playing off the Audience, and Being with the Audience

Do not confuse these two relationships. The first is the skill of the performer, the stand-up comic or the street performer. Essentially, the tone of voice, playing level and even content, varies with the audience response. Elizabethan comic actors were notorious for this. Shakespeare, in Hamlet's speech to the players, asks comic actors only to say what is in their script and not to improvise. It is possible, indeed sometimes necessary and required, for an actor to hold an audience reactively by extemporizing, but it is fatal to the actor who is interpreting a script. In this case you are doing what you prepared, but with a sixth sense for the audience presence. You know intuitively when to pause, to stop and to continue. You are acting and you are *with* the audience. You are entirely in the moment, in the world, and you can often see the faces of the audience – more importantly, you can "feel" their presence, and it is this feeling that will tell you when to pause and when to go on.

Working with the Audience and Timing

The audience is the final player in the theatre event and the company of actors must allow for this. A nervous or inexperienced actor might plow through a performance as though it were a rehearsal, perhaps speaking across the laughter of the audience, where an experienced actor would simply pause or stop, picking up the dialogue instinctively as the laughter was beginning to die. This is a skill that can only be learned through the experience of performing before a live audience.

Talking to the Audience and "Sectoring"

Sometimes it is necessary to talk to the audience directly. It may be appropriate to endow them: are they hostile strangers or intimate friends? Relate to them truthfully as characters in the play. There is also a mechanical problem of focus. You must make the audience feel as though each of them is being spoken to, but you can't actually speak to each individual. The best solution is to sector your audience. Choose three or four individuals, spread through the audience, and at least halfway into the audience. Speak to them, easily and directly, giving them clear eye contact, if appropriate, without staring. All the individuals surrounding them will feel talked to. You should move easily through the audience, focusing successively on individuals so that you share yourself with the whole audience.

The Audience is Your Mirror

The audience feels exactly as you do. It is like a mirror to your moment-by-moment on-stage feelings. These are very different from your off-stage anxieties. Actors who were sick with fear in the wings are invariably cool and focused on stage. When you are on the stage, the audience mirrors your feelings. If you are confident, so are they; if you are embarrassed, so are they; if you think you are awful, you are.

The audience needs to be safe, and held in the play's world by the actor. It has no interest whatever in the actor's difficulties, or in the actor's mistakes. The audience will not know you have made a mistake unless you tell it so! Imagine always that your relationship with your audience is adult to adult. It will not protect you, like a parent, but neither will it question your right to stand on the stage, unless you do.

Stage Etiquette

It is important to get on well with everyone else involved in the production, and to understand and accept stage etiquette.

Before a Show

It goes without saying that you must always be on time for a show. Lateness in the theatre is considered a crime for obvious reasons. Usually you are expected to be at the theatre by "the half," that is 35 minutes before the curtain goes up. The stage manager will expect to check you in at this time, but you will no doubt wish to leave some extra time to warm up and prepare yourself. Konstantin Stanislavsky, the Russian director, contrasted the attitude of the great Tommaso Salvini, who used to arrive at the theatre with hours to spare, with the mediocre actor who rushes in at the last minute. Stanislavsky's point was that Salvini was great enough to know just how much work had to be done before a performance.

Your body must be alert, your voice warm, you must recover a specific awareness of the physical and psychological qualities of the character you are playing, and you must be in the mood to enter the world of the play. This work exists irrespective of the size of your part. It is said that there are no small parts, only small actors! Carefully plan out your preparation.

Suggest, or at least support, the idea of a company warm-up, where the whole company warms up together. Ten minutes is sufficient and can make a great difference to the quality of communication during performance.

Allow yourself at least ten minutes before curtain-up to calm yourself and focus your concentration. During this time, you should not disturb other actors, nor should others disturb you. This is especially important before dress runs and early performances where the whole cast is nervous. Do not give way to your nerves by fussing.

You cannot avoid nervousness; it is an important aspect of your performance, but you can avoid unnecessary anxiety by methodically checking each practical aspect of your job before each performance. Have a simple list of jobs that you can check off. Check your costume. Check all props that you use. Check that they are in position on the props table. Check that any "practical" (working) prop that you use is actually working! Do not try to be responsible for the work of others. This is unprofessional and very annoying. Do your own work, and assume that you are working with a company of responsible, capable adults.

In the Dressing Room

Be self-sufficient and do not rely on others to supply your needs. Have a properly equipped make-up box and an "emergency kit," which should include safety pins of various sizes, some sewing needles with a light and a dark thread, a small roll of adhesive tape, a small pair of scissors, a length of elastic and some elastic bands.

In a communal dressing room, respect the privacy of others and do not impose unnecessarily – other actors may also be preparing. If you incline to mood swings, do not "dump" your mood into the space. It is disturbing and annoying to have to put up with someone's anger, anxiety or overwhelming joy when you are about to go on stage.

During the Show

Avoid playing the previous show. All audiences are different, and each will respond in a different way. Never judge the audience by the previous audience, but learn to accept that each moment is created afresh by each new audience. Avoid commenting on the audience or on how the show's going while you are in performance. You should have the same attitude to your own mistakes and those of others during the show. You require professional compassion, which is the the ability to let the error go and get on with the show.

The Transforming Actor

Although she has become a "star' of film and television, Diana Rigg remains a classical stage actress of great versatility. She has created memorable roles in the classical Greek, Shakespearean, French neoclassical and English Restoration traditions. She excels in understated ironic comedy. This was exploited as a cliché in the 1960s cult television series, *The Avengers*, but used to great effect in Tom Stoppard's *Jumpers* (1972) and *Night and Day* (1978).

A restrained, delicate and heartbreaking view of Cleopatra in **All for Love** *(1991), which portrays a world of neoclassical morals.*

Raw feeling pours through the "mask" of this larger-than-human woman in a 1972 production of **Medea**.

In **Who's Afraid of Virginia Woolf?** *(1996), the emotional experience of the actress enriches her portrayal of this realistic character.*

The World
of the
Play

Introduction

The first part of this book describes the way actors work on themselves as living "instruments," and the process whereby the actor brings to life the words of a text. This part of the book reveals the imaginative world in which this journey of discovery takes place.

In a modern production, the world of the play is a matter for the director. The director must imagine a world where the acting style, the visual impact of costume and set, the sound, the music and the relationship between the action and the audience are consistent with each other. The director's vision must be conveyed to the cast early in the rehearsal process, with the actors perhaps being given the chance to explore and discover the acting style required for the imaged production.

The actor must connect with the world of the play not only intellectually but also emotionally, with his or her feelings and instinct. Often the actor only really "hooks in" to the play at the last minute when the sound, lighting, make-up and costume suddenly heighten the sensory impact of the world in which the play is enacted. The actor should be fed with sensation, ideas and images throughout rehearsal – the world of the play is always uncharted territory, since the circumstances of any given production are unique.

The world of a play consists of many artificial elements that together comprise the imaginative form of the production. For example, the authors' view of humanity may be an important element. Racine creates a world where physical contact is unthinkable, so that desire must be articulated in a barely controlled stream of verbal images. Shakespeare, on the other hand, gives us a world in which each object has symbolic resonance and value, so it's easy to move from the mundane to the spiritual – they inform each other. Chekhov shows us a world in which everybody lies about their feelings. In the world of Shaw, every character is a highly articulate philosopher. You can see from these examples that even apparently realistic plays, such as those of Chekhov, are subject to the artificial form of the writer's style.

The writer's social assumptions are also important to actors if they are to understand the significance of decisions made by their characters. In our age, traditional social roles are often seen as disintegrating and this, combined with a whirlwind of technological change, makes our society perhaps different from earlier ones. When researching the world of past societies, it is especially important to be sensitive to attitudes toward womanhood and manhood, and to the accompanying notions of honor and dishonor, duty, responsibility and dignity. Imagine yourself swept back a hundred years into the past. The buildings, streets and many physical features of the community would be identical, except that the buildings would be inhabited by people whose habits, moral code and social ritual were entirely foreign to us.

Another feature of the world of the play is the tradition of the form. All playwrights develop or attack the tradition of the form in which they write. I have chosen four traditions, each of which contains a galaxy of worlds. In each tradition there are, however, issues that will inevitably arise for the actor. In tragedy, for example, the issue is *volume*. The actor must feel part of an action that is larger than life, and on a path that is inevitable and irresistible. In comedy, the issue is *velocity*. Characters must be driven to speak before they think, never quite having time to engage with their reasoning faculties. In Epic, the issue is *playfulness*, the ability to shift easily from dialogue to song, to aside and to soliloquy, thereby manipulating the actor/audience relationship with the changes. For Realism, the quality of *empathy* is essential, so that the audience can feel that they are eavesdropping on real life.

111

Chapter 5

Comedy

Man and Animal

In ancient society, comedy had an important place in religious life. By reminding humans of their animal nature and by lampooning social pretentiousness, comic writers and actors helped individuals to avoid hubris – pride against the gods.

The ancient Greeks had social and religious uses for comedy. The *komos* was a procession in which dancers, sporting huge leather bellies, buttocks and penises, advertised and inaugurated the winter drama festival. Comic actors lampooned the tendency of self-important humans to keep secret their animal needs. The festival was a spiritual antidote to hubris, which is pride against the gods. It was also an affirmation that, whatever the foibles and idiocies of society, humans still had to perform animal functions and, particularly, produce the next generation. Thus we have the comic tradition of sexual desire thwarted by social convention. Sexual attraction finally achieves its end, often by chance or through unbelievable coincidence, when the right couple pairs up.

Plautus (*c.* 254–184 BC), the Roman clown turned comic dramatist, used comic types, such as the Cunning Slave, the Bragging Soldier and the Miser. He created complicated plots in which these simple types could function, and they satirized life in the city.

The ancient Italian *commedia dell'arte* also used comic types, and employed knockabout physical routines with stock characters. These characters usually had a fixed idea – for food, sex or money – and behaved in an entirely predictable way if these needs were triggered by their situation. This made the characters predictable to the audience, though not to themselves, and so the audience laughed at them from a position of superiority.

The French playwright Molière (1622–73) and the Italian playwright Carlo Goldoni (1707–93) were both heavily influenced by *commedia dell'arte*. Molière attracted the literate middle classes to his plays, which combined *commedia*

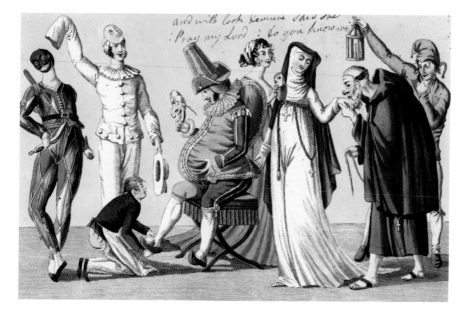

Traditional masks and costume for commedia dell'arte characters complemented traditional gestures, routines and accents. Men and women (unusually) played together.

Oscar Wilde's comedies of manners (this is a scene from The Importance of Being Earnest) *celebrate the very society they criticize.*

knockabout with brilliant dialogue. Goldoni's *Servant of Two Masters* consists of *commedia* routines in script form.

It is crucial in comedy that the audience is kept on the edge of what is safe. If it is too safe it is boring, and if it is too dangerous the audience may be offended. It is therefore necessary to hold the audience in a state of dangerous balance. The comedies of manners by Oscar Wilde (1854–1900), for example, make fun of the social pretensions that the audience share, but the criticism is balanced because the characters who mimic us seem so like us – witty and charming with an admirable facility for language!

The balance of criticism and flattery is found in Wilde and survives into the twentieth century in Tom Stoppard's sparkling dialogue. Elsewhere the comic landscape has darkened, perhaps foreshadowed in the nineteenth century and early twentieth century by the French dramatist Georges Feydeau (1862–1921), whose farces, tearing along at a breathtaking pace, threaten at every moment to puncture the gilded bubble of bourgeois family life and plunge the world into nightmare. Modern tragi-comic playwrights, such as John Guare and Terry Johnson, are in the dark comic tradition of Feydeau, as was Joe Orton (1933–67).

Comedy of ideas: Tom Stoppard's dialogue is distinctive for its sparkling wit and brilliant manipulation of language. Rosencrantz and Guildenstern are Dead *is one of his earlier plays.*

Molière (Jean-Baptiste Poquelin, 1622-73)

Molière raised comedy to a great art.

Molière was a French actor-manager and playwright. After a brief and disastrous attempt to establish an acting company in Paris, he emerged from a debtor's prison to join a traveling company that included the famous Béjart family, with whom he had also been previously involved. During the next 15 years he learned his trade, heavily influenced by the *commedia dell'arte* troups. In 1658 he secured a command performance before Louis XIV. Molière's comedy was a great success, and his company became established in Paris.

Molière remained in Paris for the next 15 years until his death at the early age of 51, transforming French comedy by combining the physical vigor of *commedia* with sparkling, witty dialogue. This appealed to a broad audience that included the rising middle class as well as the aristocracy.

Molière married Armande Béjart and created many of his female lead roles for her. These include Elmire in *Tartuffe* (1664), Célimène in *The Misanthrope* (1666), Elise in *The Miser* (1668), Lucille in *The Aspiring Gentleman* (1670) and Armande in *The Learned Ladies* (1672). His career did not meet with unmitigated success. *Tartuffe* and *Don Juan* were both attacked and banned by the clergy, and Molière himself alternated between high favor and disgrace at court. Ceaseless work took its toll, and Molière had mainly given up acting several years before his death. His last play was *The Hypochondriac* (1673).

This is farce at the climax of *Tartuffe* – Molière's rigorous attack on religious hypocrisy.

Molière's great contribution to the theatre was to make comedy respectable, and to give it acknowledged, worthwhile themes. Up to this point in history, comedy had been associated with disreputable low life but, after Molière, it was seen to be capable of assuming the same importance as tragedy.

The Hypochondriac *was the last of Molière's great obsessive characters.*

The Miser by Molière

Comic characters are distinguished by simple rigidity of character. In Molière, characters such as the Aspiring Gentleman, the Hypochondriac, Don Juan and the Miser have a single motivation, respectively status, fear of disease, sex and money. Their names tell the audience what moves them. These characters must not be complex, and must behave as the audience expects them to. The Miser must always become emotionally distraught at the thought of losing or spending money. This thought must take the character to the edge of control, and it is this dangerous edge that makes us, the audience, laugh from a comfortable position of superiority. To achieve this reaction, the characters themselves must go to extremes, making the language as physical as possible. In the following scene from Act 4, Harpagon (the Miser) has just discovered that his cash-box has been stolen. He is apoplectic with rage and grief.

I have broken down this famous speech into physical activities. I have suggested (in bold type within square brackets) how the text moves through different activities and shifts of mood. The activities must change quickly and abruptly, and must be supported by sudden, inner compulsions that make the body move.

(Beats up his arm)

"Give me my money back you scoundrel!"

"Who's that?"

"Is he there?"

"Is he here?"

"They've cut my throat; they've taken my money!"

"I'm murdered!"

"Thieves! Robbers!"

116

"I'm going out of my mind!"

"Oh dear, my dear, darling money . . ."

"I'm dead."

"Will nobody bring me to life again by giving me my beloved money back . . ."

"Eh? What d'ye say?"

"I'll demand justice."

"Myself included!"

HARPAGON

(*Calling "Stop, thief!" in the garden. He enters hatless*).
[**Shouting at the audience**] Thieves! Robbers! Assassins!
Murderers! Justice! [**Grabbing hold of himself**] Merciful
Heavens! I'm done for! [**Falling to his knees**] I'm
murdered! [**To himself**] They've cut my throat; they've
taken my money! [**Leaping up and scanning the
audience**] Whoever can it be? Where's he gone to? Where is
he now? Where is he hiding? How can I find him?
[**Suddenly running away**] Which way shall I go?
[**Suddenly stopping**] Which way shan't I go? [**Suddenly
turning left**] Is he here? [**Suddenly turning right**] Is he
there? [**Seeing his own arm**] Who's that? Stop! (*Catching
his own arm*) [**Holds his arm still**] Give me my money
back, you scoundrel! [**He mercilessly beats up his arm,
suddenly feeling intense pain . . .**] Ah! It's me! I'm going
out of my mind! I don't know where I am or who I am or
what I'm doing. [**Falling to his knees; suddenly
sentimental**] Oh dear, my dear, darling money, my beloved,
they've taken you away from me and now you are gone I
have lost my strength, my joy and my consolation. [**To
himself**] It's all over with me. There's nothing left for me to
do in the world. [**Clutching his heart**] I can't go on living
without you. It's the finish. I can't bear any more. I'm
dying; [**Shuts his eyes**] I'm dead – [**He keels over**] and
buried. [**Loudly, so that the robber, if hiding nearby,
would hear him**] Will nobody bring me to life again by
giving me my beloved money back or telling me who has
taken it? [**Pause. Suddenly leaping up and opening his
eyes**] Eh? What d'ye say? [**Sad again**] There's nobody
there![...] [**Furious**] I'll demand justice. I'll have everyone
in the house put to the torture, menservants, maidservants,
son, daughter, everyone. Myself included!

Obviously, a technical facility is required in the speech on page 117 because Harpagon is not thinking logically but responding to impulses which, if he thought about them for two seconds, he would see are ridiculous. Speed and clarity of action are therefore required and must be practiced technically so that eventually they can be performed as a response to a flow of impulsive, frightened thoughts – the inner life of the character.

Work in pairs. One partner speaks the text, while the other creates a pattern of movement as I have suggested in the speech on page 117 in the bold type.

Creating a Pattern of Movement

First, let the words lead and the actions follow, until a pattern is established.

Next, play the text as it should be played, with the speech following the actions. Harpagon moves impulsively, and then explains to himself or to the audience what has happened to him. Then work at creating tempo.

Make the changes clear, clean and swift. You have no time for thought. Rehearse this piece in the style of farce, which has a quick pace and heightened physicalness.

Next, play the whole speech yourself, working until you have mastered the psychophysical flow of activities. Finally, create an appropriate animal character for Harpagon. Now try to play the piece "in character," and remember that Harpagon is 60 years old (see right).

Establish the weight, tempo and center of the animal (see page 39).

Use the "essences" of weight, tempo and animal center in the characters.

Use costume elements to dress what has been physically established.

Find the "class" of the character through the essences and elements.

Replay Harpagon in character.

Neil Simon (1927-   )

Neil Simon is an American dramatist, and was the most successful playwright of the 1960s. Born in New York, he began his career with his brother, writing comic material for personalities of radio and television as well as comic sketches for Broadway shows.

His first hit comedy was *Come Blow Your Horn* (1961), followed by the musical *Little Me* (1962), *Barefoot in the Park* (1963) and *The Odd Couple* (1965). During the 1970s, Simon's writing became more reflective and serious; his popularity decreased accordingly. *The Gingerbread Lady* (1970), which dealt with alcoholism, was rejected by audiences, and likewise *The Good Doctor* (1973), which was adapted from Chekhov short stories.

Simon's subsequent career has been checkered, including hits such as *California Suite* (1976) and failures such as *Fools* (1981). The recent upturn in his fortunes comprises the innovative and successful autobiographical *Brighton Beach Memoirs* (1983), *Biloxi Blues* (1984), which won a Tony award, and a successful revival of *The Odd Couple*, with the title roles rewritten for two women.

Inspired situation comedy: Simon's range takes in the purely commercial and the art form. This scene is from The Odd Couple.

Neil Simon is a writer of hit plays for whom critical acclaim has come slowly.

Status

The body withdraws.

LOW STATUS

A compulsion to look back.

Irregular tempo.

If tragedy concentrates on the highest qualities of humanity, then comedy concentrates on the lowest.

In tragedy, human beings are in the company of gods whereas, in comedy, they are in the company of animals. All animals, including humans, indulge in status play. This is a way of creating space for ourselves by making physical signals. It is the reason why we don't bump into each other on a crowded street – we know instinctively whether others will or will not give way to us. We can play low status by sending out signals that we are deferential and harmless, or high status by imposing our presence on the space. Either technique is equally effective, creating a pecking order that places us in the spiritual company of chickens!

Status transactions are taking place continually, irrespective of the actual dialogue, however cultured and high-flown.

Stillness.

HIGH STATUS

Elements of high-status play are regular physical tempo, smooth movement, stillness, long pauses and measured speech rhythms, no deference in the eyes and level eye contact with no compulsion to look at your partner. There is an expansive use of space, with the chest and belly exposed. Elements of low-status play are irregular tempo and a quick, stuttering action of the body and in speech. Pauses are filled with activity and there is deference in the eyes with a compulsion to look back at your partner. The body withdraws from space; shoulders are rounded, protecting the chest and belly.

Smooth movement.

Level eye contact.

Gary (right) slightly higher than Christian (left).

Christian's tempo is quick, he doesn't take up space.

Christian continues to relax, Gary to crumple.

Gary's tempo quickens, some deference in the eyes.

Gary remains still.

Exercise

Practicing High and Low Status

Working with a partner, have a conversation in which you place your status a little above or below that of your partner. Initially, concentrate on single physical activities: the eyes, movement of the head and rhythm of speech. Notice and yield to the emotional effects of these transactions.

Christian begins to relax, holding eye contact.

Steady eye contact makes status play between them close.

Christian's tempo slows and becomes nearer to Gary's.

121

"Nevertheless, I'm well over sixty, Frosine."

"Well, what's sixty?"

"I never saw you looking so sprightly."

"Really?"

"Goodness me, how well you are looking . . ."

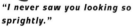

Exercise

An Extract from *The Miser*

Play the following fragment from *The Miser*, Act 2, in which Frosine, a professional matchmaker, is trying to pair off Harpagon with Mariane, who is in love with his son. Her technique is to raise Harpagon's status by elevating him and lowering herself. My comments are in bold type within square brackets.

FROSINE [Her breathing light and quick, as though taken by surprise] Goodness me, how well you are looking – the very picture of health!

HARPAGON [Slowing down] Who? Me!

FROSINE [Fluttering her eyes, as though embarrassed] I never saw you looking so fresh and sprightly.

HARPAGON [Opening his chest and belly to the space] Really?

FROSINE Why, you've never looked so young in your life. [Putting herself down] I know fellows of twenty-five who are not half as youthful as you are.

HARPAGON [Slow and patronizing] Nevertheless, I'm well over sixty, Frosine.

FROSINE [Quick and impulsive] Well, what's sixty? What of it? It's the very flower of one's age. You are just coming to the prime of life.

Exercise

Playing Parts of Different Status

To get the feel of the different states, play both parts on your own!

"How well you are looking."

"Who? Me!"

"I never saw you looking so fresh . . . ."

"Really?"

I know fellows who are not half as youthful . . ."

Nevertheless, . . . Frosine."

Dario Fo (1926-   )

Dario Fo is an Italian actor, director and playwright, and most of his career has been associated with his wife, the actress and playwright Franca Rame. He began as a farceur, using the techniques and strategies of popular street and fairground theatre, and became popular with bourgeois audiences for his satire.

Fo had established a national reputation as a satirist by the 1960s. By 1968, he and Franca were running a company that specialized in comedy. The events of 1968 caused them to abandon "bourgeois" theatre and, with a short-lived company called Nuova Scena, they attempted to take theatre to working-class populations, playing in clubs and in the open air. Fo wrote a number of didactic pieces; during the same period he created the celebrated *Mistero buffo* (the Comic Mysteries), in which he used the medieval mystery form that strings biblical allegories, fables and sketches together into an epic event. Fo performed all the parts, exploring the two ancient acting traditions of the "jongleur" – the subversive fool of medieval times – and the masked and clowning *commedia* actor. In 1970, the Fos split from the Italian Communist Party and formed another company, La Commune, for which Fo wrote his best-known plays, including *Accidental Death of an Anarchist* (1970) and *Can't Pay? Won't Pay!* (1974).

Can't Pay? Won't Pay! Fo's most popular play outside Italy, focuses on the raw farce of civil disobedience.

Chapter 6

Tragedy

God and Man

Tragedy explores the human struggle to relate to God or fate or, more recently, to a predestined psychological pattern of life. Its ancient religious roots lie in the idea of sacrifice.

The word tragedy comes from the Greek *tragos* (goat) and *ôdê* (song) and thus means "goat song", which was the anthem sung to the sacrificial animal at festivals dedicated to the god Dionysius in Athens in the fifth century BC. The element of sacrifice is central to an understanding of classical tragedy, in which the hero takes the place of the sacrificial victim. Because ritual killing was known only to high priests, it took place in secret, away from spectators. Violent action is therefore never seen in these plays, but is reported by onlookers, messengers or the chorus. The audiences at classical tragedies already knew the plot, but wanted to

The ancient Greek theatre of Epidaurus. The acoustics are so perfect that 20,000 people can hear a pin drop!

see how the playwright would use it to explore the relationship between the hero and the gods.

The Greek philosopher Aristotle (384–322 BC), writing 200 years after these plays were first produced, observed that unity of form in playwriting contributed to the force of tragedy. *Oedipus Rex* by the dramatist Sophocles (*c.* 495–406 BC) came nearest to this perfect form in his opinion. Aristotle suggested that the characters in tragedy should be "elevated" types (kings, queens and demi-gods), and that they should be essentially good with one

Oedipus Rex *is often quoted as a perfect example of a tragedy.*

In neoclassical drama such as Racine's **Andromache,** *the servant acts as "confidante", becoming the "midwife" of the heroine's agonized imagination.*

weakness of character – the tragic flaw that precipitates disaster upon them.

Seventeenth-century French "new" or neoclassical playwrights used Aristotle's observations as though they were strict rules. The neoclassical tragedies of Racine (1639–99), for example, make strict use of a single location and plot, a 24-hour time-span, no on-stage action, classical mythological characters for heroes, and employ Alexandrine couplets (12 syllables, with 6 stresses to the line; rhymed in pairs) as spoken verse.

William Shakespeare (1564–1616), and other English Elizabethan playwrights, ignored classical tragic form. They used many locations, an arbitrary time-span, and they mixed comic scenes into the tragic plot. Dialogue was mixed with music, songs, dances, stand-up comedy, battle scenes and processions. Newly discovered iambic pentameter (10 syllables, with 5 stresses to the line) was used for elevated thought, while couplets and prose serve for low-life scenes.

The Elizabethan tragic universe described the disruption and attempted restitution of symmetry and order within a Christian framework. Thought and speech moved easily between the domestic, the physical, the political and the universal because, poetically, they stood for each other. Human beings were at the center of the universe while the sun, planets and stars encircled them, playing the ethereal "music of the spheres." This one could only hear when the human body had ceased its noise and was silent, usually at the moment of death. The Elizabethan model of a universal pattern gave way in later Jacobean work to a darker vision, as if playwrights intuitively felt the storm clouds of the English Civil War approaching. Under Queen Elizabeth I (1558–1603) theatre had been a popular pastime but, under James I (1603–1625), it became an expensive indoor activity for bored aristocrats. The universe was shown as fragmenting, and heroes died confused "in a mist." Many of Shakespeare's great plays are of this later period.

Domestic, or bourgeois, tragedy explored the idea that ordinary people could have tragic lives. Invented in London in 1731 by the now forgotten playwright George Lillo (1693–1739), the form quickly set Europe aflame. In this type of tragedy the universe was seen as essentially moral and characters suffered through their moral weaknesses. The plays were highly emotional and eventually degenerated into melodrama. At the end of a 1781 performance of *The Robbers* by the German playwright and poet Friedrich von Schiller (1759–1805), total strangers were said to embrace each other in floods of tears, and men and women, overcome by emotion, fainted in the aisles while making their exit.

Revenge, incest and cynical betrayal signify a collapse of values in the Jacobean charnel house. Webster's **The White Devil** *is a typical example.*

Waiting for Godot by Samuel Beckett (1906–89) is an exploration of the shattered spiritual landscape particular to the twentieth century. The sometimes tragic and sometimes comic anti-heroic protagonists edge towards realizing that there is no God, no order and no meaning to hold on to outside themselves. The US dramatist Arthur Miller (1915–   ) is an example of a modern playwright still able to write within a moral framework. For him the struggle is to hold on to one's humanity. Miller says:

The tragic feeling is evoked in us when we are in the presence of a character who is ready to lay down his life, if need be, to secure one thing – his sense of personal dignity . . . Tragedy, then, is the consequence of a man's total compulsion to evaluate himself justly.

Waiting for Godot *– in a cruel and arbitrary universe modern man's life alternates between boredom and pain.*

William Shakespeare (1564-1616)

Very little is known about Shakespeare, who is the greatest playwright of all time. He was born in Stratford-upon-Avon in 1564, the son of a glover, and his life falls into three main periods. His first 20 years were spent at his place of birth; during this period he married Anne Hathaway and had two children before leaving for London. In the second phase of his life he had a 25-year career as actor, playwright and shareholder in the Globe Theatre. He finally retired to Stratford where he became a wealthy member of the local gentry.

Shakespeare wrote plays during the late sixteenth and early seventeenth century for a London-based company of actors whom he knew personally. Companies played in the middle of the afternoon, in a noisy atmosphere and in broad daylight to all sections of the London community, most of whom were illiterate. Sometimes they had as many as 20 plays in the repertoire. Women did not act, only men and boys. The boys were apprenticed to craft actors and used in the female roles while their voices remained unbroken. The craft of acting consisted of mime (the language of gesture), declamation (effective delivery of speech) and an understanding of the conventions of text. Thus a boy could "play" a part like Cleopatra, much as a talented child could play a violin concerto – by formally learning the score. There were a number of "boys' companies," rivals to companies such as Shakespeare's, where all parts were played by choirboys.

If you were an Elizabethan actor in a play by Shakespeare you might have signed a three-year contract

Hamlet is one of the greatest and most widely performed of Shakespeare's plays.

agreeing to pay a shilling fine if you turned up to rehearsal late, three shillings if you were late for the actual show and ten shillings if four of the company agreed that when the play started you were drunk! You would usually wear some expensive contemporary clothes as costume. Since Shakespeare's actors were the Lord Chamberlain's company, they would probably wear his cast-offs. The actors would not get a script in case they sold it to another company. There was no copyright law, so scripts were locked away to be used only by the prompter. Instead, the actors would get a "side" or cue script with only their own words on it and their cue line. There would be very little rehearsal time and no director, only the prompter who would sit on the stage during the performance and prompt in full voice. The stage action would be gleaned from the text, and actors would be trained to do this. After preparation and line learning, the actors came together to rehearse entrances and exits. Offstage would be the platt, a large prompt board that carried the plot of the play, and some directorial commentary, which cued entrances. The actors would listen intently to hear and respond to their cues, and the action would develop spontaneously as the players responded and followed the path of words according to the stage convention. There was no stage scenery and no attempt to convince the audience that they were actually in Verona or Denmark – Shakespeare never set foot out of England – nor to recreate the past, which is why there are clocks in *Julius Caesar*!

The language Shakespeare wrote was never meant to be appreciated as literature or poetry. Every full stop, comma, break in line, eccentric spelling and capital letter in the text was a *choice* made not in the service of literature, but in the service of the actor. The pattern of words on the page told the actor not only what to say, but also what to do. In the First Folio, the version Shakespeare actually wrote, the apparently eccentric use of capital letters and the phonetic spellings are actually telling the actor how the words *sound*. Much of this information has been wiped out by scholarly attempts to turn Shakespeare's text into respectable poetry, but today there is a welcome trend back to the First Folio, the clearest version for the actor. Whatever version an actor uses, the general rule with Shakespeare is to *obey the text*. If characters say they are furious, in love or lying, then they are! There is no subtext. Stage directions are also contained in the text, and the emotional pitch of the scene is implied by the use of poetry or prose.

The verse form used by Shakespeare was predominantly blank verse. It was a breakthrough when Christopher Marlowe established this pattern in *Tamburlaine the Great* (1587) because blank verse resembles the normal patterns of English speech more than any other poetic form except unrhymed free verse. Shakespeare was able to develop this form freely, finding a wide range in his plays that included lyrical ecstasy, knockabout comedy and towering fury.

This production of Romeo and Juliet *captures the essence of Shakespearean drama: action and poetry on a bare stage.*

Shakespeare on Acting

Excerpt from Hamlet's speech to the actors

(Act 3, Scene 1)

HAMLET ... Suit the action to the word, the word to the action, with this special observance; that you o'erstep not the modesty of Nature: for any thing so overdone, is from the purpose of playing, whose end both at the first and now, was and is, to hold, as 'twere, the mirror up to Nature; to show Virtue her own feature, Scorn her own image, and the very age and body of the time, his form and pressure.

A dramatic version of Lady Macbeth.

Macbeth by William Shakespeare

These sample texts are taken from *Macbeth*, Act 1, Scene 7, which begins with Macbeth's great soliloquy in which his resolution to kill King Duncan fails completely. By the end of the scene, however, Lady Macbeth has shamed, cajoled and seduced him back on to his murderous path.

Making the Text Physical

In this sort of text language is like a series of shapes sculpted from words. The words themselves have a physicalness and energy, and the actor's job is literally to embody the language, and to get it into the muscles and bones. There is, of course, no point in doing this if you don't understand what you're saying. You must use a well-annotated text and rigorously look up any word you don't know.

"I would, while it was smiling in my face . . ."

". . . smiling in my face."

". . . smiling smiling . . . smiling . . ."

"Have plucked my nipple from his boneless gums."

"Have plucked . . . Have plucked . . ."

"And dashed the brains out . . ."

"Dashed . . . dashed . . ."

"Had I so sworn . . ."

Exercise

Dancing the Speech

Once you are sure of the meaning and shape of the speech, try dancing it. You can forget psychological action altogether, and treat the words and phrases as objects, or as living things that have weight, tempo and direction. Let the phrases move your body and be particularly aware of the shifts in weight and tempo, a heavy phrase transforming into something light and quick, for example. Repeat phrases that move you, working them into your body.

Here the actress rehearses another speech from the same scene.

LADY MACBETH
I would, while it was smiling in my face,
Have plucked my nipple from his boneless gums,
And dashed the brains out, had I so sworn as you
Have done to this.

Breaking up the Text

Break up the text into whole thoughts. Breathe at the end of each thought, and let each thought end with a slightly rising inflexion (the vocal note rises slightly). For example, I have broken up a fragment of the dialogue in this way. Breathe when you see ★.

You see that you need not breathe at the end of each line, and that by marking the breaths, you discover the shape and rhythm of the thought in the text.

"We will proceed no further . . ."

"Was the hope drunk . . .?"

Making the Relationship Physical

Use a rope about 3yd (3m) long and play this scene with the rope tied around your waists. Let the action of each beat of the scene be physically expressed through the rope. You may hold it taut if you feel you are dominating your partner, wrap it tenderly around your partner, or pull your partner towards you.

"Hath it slept since?"

"Such I account thy love."

"Art thou afeard . . .?"

"And live a coward in thine own esteem."

MACBETH
We will proceed no further in this business.
★ He hath honoured me of late, ★ and I have bought
Golden opinions from all sorts of people
Which would be worn now in their newest gloss, ★
Not cast aside so soon. ★
LADY MACBETH
Was the hope drunk
Wherein you dressed yourself? ★ Hath it slept since?
And wakes it now to look so green and pale
At what it did so freely? ★ From this time
Such I account thy love. ★ Art thou afeard
To be the same in thine own act and valour
As thou art in desire? ★ Wouldst thou have that
Which thou esteem'st the ornament of life,
And live a coward in thine own esteem,
Letting "I dare not" wait upon "I would",
Like the poor cat i'th' adage? ★
MACBETH
Prithee, peace! ★

Different Acting Possibilities

A great scene from a great tragedy has many layers and many possibilities. The director will, of course, lead you into and through the world of the particular production in which you are involved but you, as the actor, must explore all possibilities. You should be aware of the range of options, moment by moment, and never settle for the first solution that comes into your mind.

Here are some playing "angles" for Act 1, Scene 7 of *Macbeth*.

(1) *The domestic syntax.*
"Was the hope drunk . . .?"

(2) *The sexual syntax.*
"Was the hope drunk Wherein you dressed yourself?"

Exercise

Exploring the Syntax of the Scene

1 The domestic syntax. Play the scene with Lady Macbeth as an unbearable "scold" and Macbeth as the henpecked husband.
2 The sexual syntax. Lady Macbeth treats Macbeth's fear of murder as sexual impotence.
3 The syntax of madness. Reverse the actual dynamic of the scene to show Lady Macbeth as emotionally unstable and Macbeth's resolution to kill Duncan as a way of comforting her.
4 The supernatural syntax. Lady Macbeth bewitches Macbeth with the false logic of Satan.

(3) *The syntax of madness.*
"Was the hope drunk Wherein you dressed yourself?"   *"Hath it slept since?"*

(4) *The supernatural syntax*

"Was the hope drunk . . .?"

These various angles on the scene are not necessarily how you will actually play it in performance. They are a means of exploration. You could equally well play the scene with a strong physical condition: for example, in extreme cold. Each new focus of concentration gives texture to your performance because your body will remember the text as played through in these various ways.

"Hath it slept since?"

"Hath it slept since?"

"Was the hope drunk . . .?"

"Hath it slept since?"

"Hath it slept since?"

"Wherein you dressed yourself?"

Tadashi Suzuki (1939-   )

Tadashi Suzuki is a Japanese director, playwright and theorist. His career began in the 1960s with a concerted attempt to replace text-based theatre with actor-based theatre. His play *And then, and then, what the?* (1968) used traditional Japanese *kabuki* theatre to explore non-Stanislavskian acting. Suzuki would continue to experiment with Eastern technique in the production of Western classic texts. His company was called the Waseda Little Theatre, and its first major success was *On the Dramatic Passions II* (1970), which used Western and *kabuki* scenes in a surreal collage.

In 1976 he relocated his company to a thatched-roof farmhouse in the tiny, remote mountain village of Toga. The 40-member company now spends the summer in Toga. Here he developed the "Suzuki method," which combines traditional Japanese *No* and *kabuki* technique with martial arts to produce a rigorous and physical actor discipline.

Suzuki is known for his interpretation of classical tragedy. His innovative classical Greek productions include Euripedes' *Trojan Women* (1974), *The Bacchae* (1978) and *Clytemnestra* (1980), which was a collage of five tragedies. Suzuki's repertoire expanded in the mid-1970s. His collage dramas included *Don Hamlet* (1973), Chekhov's *Three Sisters* and *Night and Clock*, which combined scenes from *Macbeth* with *kabuki* text.

In 1984 the Waseda Little Theatre became SCOT, the Suzuki Company of Toga.

Chapter 7

Epic *and* *Storytelling* *Theatre*

The Actor as Storyteller

In epic or storytelling theatre, the actor relates directly to the audience. He or she may play several roles, but it is the task of telling the story that is most important.

The epic form of theatre is the opposite of perfect tragedy as defined by Aristotle (see Tragedy, page 125). Epic is wide-ranging, taking place in many locations. It may span many years – a person's lifetime and many generations. Comedy and tragedy are mixed together, perhaps with many subplots. There is no theatrical unity of form, but there is narrative unity. Perhaps a main character's story is told, or a formal pattern of apparently disparate stories together create a coherent epic tale.

The earliest known example of epic storytelling in Western tradition is Homer's *Odyssey*, which tells the adventures of Odysseus returning to Ithaca after the sack of Troy. If we imagine the storyteller of old recounting this story using narrative and song, and demonstrating incidents in the tale through imitating the characters and acting out the scenes, we have the predecessor close to the epic actor.

This style of acting requires flexibility, a range of technical skills and a great facility for relating directly to the audience. The actor may play several roles in one production. The telling of the story is the most important task. The playwright and the players usually have a clear "angle" on the story, sometimes going so far as to draw a moral from

Mother Courage's cart is the focus for Brecht's episodic exploration of the human cost of war and profiteering.

it. In Brecht, this process is refined to a specific political endeavor, and the actors are expected to believe personally in the message of his story.

Plays that combine storytelling with epic play construction include the large-scale medieval mystery plays. These cycles, which are actually a large number of playlets, take in the whole span of the biblical story from the Creation to the Fall and redemption of mankind. Comic and tragic in turn, using song and dance, physical routines, spectacular stunts, processions and narrative, it was certainly epic in length, sometimes lasting for three weeks!

Many elements of epic form can be found in the writings of the Elizabethan playwrights who succeeded the medieval playwrights, including Shakespeare. The structure of Elizabethan tragedy is in every way epic, being episodic, wide-ranging in terms of time and place, and combining plot with subplot, tragedy and comedy. All of these features are found in the works of Shakespeare. For example, Shakespeare's use of a storyteller includes "Rumour" in *Henry IV, Part 2* ("*Enter* Rumour, *painted full of tongues*"). Rumour is an old-fashioned medieval storyteller, while "Chorus" in *Henry V* has a more personal and subtle relationship with the audience.

Bertolt Brecht's work is in the medieval, Elizabethan and Jacobean tradition. His many adaptations and revisions of these sixteenth- and seventeenth-century plays testify to his fascination with this period of writing. Brecht was also interested in Eastern traditional theatre, and he demanded of his actors disciplined physical expression as well as the ability to cope with a wide range of narrative techniques asking that, even in those of his plays which do not include a storyteller, the actor should "show" the story as well as "be" the character.

A very popular modern form of theatre is the adaptation of stories and novels into plays. *The Mahabharata*, adapted from the world's longest poem, written in Sanskrit and in the Indian tradition known as the epic, was produced by Peter Brook in 1988. It is a fine example of the adapted book being used, which is now so popular as narrative theatre. Similarly, the great success in the UK and USA of David Edgar's adaptation of *Nicholas Nickleby* for the Royal Shakespeare Company, and Shared Experience's 1996 production of *War and Peace* for the London National Theatre, testify to the growing importance of storytelling-as-performance in the modern theatre.

The Mahabharata *is an ancient well of epic narrative. Here Eastern and Western storytelling traditions combine.*

The Actor and the Ever-present Audience

In epic theatre, the audience does not peer through the "fourth wall" of the proscenium arch into the world of the play. In the epic world, the audience is always present by convention. It may be ignored for long periods because the characters on stage are totally engaged with each other, but in each moment of the play the audience is available to be talked to. Brecht favored lights directed on the audience so that the actor could clearly see their faces, and this convention is now generally adopted in narrative theatre. Asides in character allow the audience a sudden, direct intimacy, which is thrilling and engaging, especially since some crucial piece of information is often imparted which is not known to the other characters. In medieval theatre, the character of Satan spoke to the audience. He always seduced them easily, being less remote and more fun than Jesus or God. Shakespeare uses Richard III and Iago in the same way. They touch the wickedness in us and seduce us in spite of their evil.

Comic Aside.
However frantic the scene, characters can always pull out and chat to the audience. Here it is necessary to be tense and frightened in the scene, but easy and offhand with the audience.

The Intermediary.
The character describes to the audience the scene being played upstage. The audience gets the intermediary character's point of view, which may explain the plot, or the attitude of the character, or both. Only the audience and the character are privy to this information.

The Audience as "Confidant."
This is the sort of aside you find in Molière. Here the characters share their real feelings with the audience, but pose and lie to each other. The audience is the confidant of each character in turn. Only the audience sees the whole truth whereas the characters are left partly in the dark. (The fan and scarf are not strictly necessary if the characters have split-second timing and can change focus sharply enough between talking to each other and to the audience.)

Bertolt Brecht
(1898-1956)

Brecht was a German dramatist, poet, director and songwriter. He was 16 years old at the outbreak of the First World War, served as a medical orderly in 1918, and from this experience learned a life-long hatred of war.

His early plays *Baal* (1919) and *Drums in the Night* (1922) were nihilistic in attitude and expressionistic in form. They caused scandal and riot, but earned Brecht the Kleist Drama Prize in 1922.

Brecht then began to experiment with anti-illusionistic staging. His 1924 adaptation of Christopher Marlowe's *Edward II*, which used scene titles written on placards, worked as a cool analysis of the events of the play. Herbert Ihering wrote in 1926 that, "He compelled a clear and cool manner of speaking. No emotional tricks were allowed. This ensured the objective 'Epic' style."

Brecht next moved to Berlin, and worked with the Austrian director, actor and manager Max Reinhardt (1873–1943) and the German director Erwin Piscator (1893–1966). He wrote musical plays such as the *The Threepenny Opera* (1928), in

Bertolt Brecht combined the talents of writing, acting, directing and teaching.

collaboration with the musician Kurt Weill (1900–50), and *The Rise and Fall of the City of Mahagonny* (1930). Brecht also began to write "teaching plays" during this time, presenting a Marxist analysis of political events set in distant countries and historical periods so that the setting did not interfere with the argument.

Brecht was driven out of Germany by the Nazis in 1933 and went to live in Scandinavia. He wrote his greatest plays during this exile: *The Life of Galileo* (1938), *Mother Courage and her Children* (1939), *The Good Woman of Setzuan* (1940) and *The Resistible Rise of Arturo Ui* (1941) as well as *The Caucasian Chalk Circle* (1943).

Brecht settled briefly in the USA until driven

The Good Woman of Setzuan *explores the use of the mask and Eastern acting techniques.*

out by McCarthy. He returned to East Berlin after the war in 1948 where he and his wife, Helene Weigel, established a theatre company, the Berliner Ensemble. It is from this time that Brecht's reputation began to grow internationally. Although his plays are not produced with great regularity, the influence of his ideas on theatre is enormous. Much of his theory has been absorbed into modern theatre practice.

The Resistible Rise of Arturo Ui *is a parable play about Fascism.*

Helene Weigel (1900–71)

Helene Weigel was Brecht's great leading actress. She began her career in 1918 as Maria in *Woyzeck* by Georg Büchner (1813–37). She met Brecht in 1924, acting in his plays and attracting critical acclaim through her interpretation of Lady Macbeth and the servant messenger in *Oedipus Rex*. Her career was halted in 1933 when she and Brecht fled Berlin after the Riechstag fire (Brecht was fifth on the Nazi extermination list). During their period in exile she did not perform, but returned with him early in the 1950s to run the Berliner Ensemble. She recreated her definitive interpretations of the Epic Theatre roles of Vlassova in *The Mother*, and of Mother Courage. When Brecht died in 1956, she continued to run the Berliner Ensemble, mounting world tours that established his reputation postumously .

Helene Weigel was the actress who best exemplified Brecht's ideas on acting.

The Caucasian Chalk Circle by Bertolt Brecht

DESCRIPTIVE STORY

"As she was standing . . ."

Exercise

Talking to the Audience

Tell a simple story to an audience. For example, tell part of the singer's story in Scene 2 of *The Caucasian Chalk Circle*. Grusha, the serving maid, is escaping from the burning palace just after the *coup d'état* has taken place. She is about to desert the baby of the deposed governor's wife:

Next, explore the issues for the actor in this passage. First tell the story adult-to-adult, without making your audience feel younger than they are. Ask for feedback when you've finished.

1 Now combine words with gestures. First, let your gestures *describe* the story as you tell it, placing the courtyard, the gate, Grusha and the child.

". . . she heard or thought she heard . . ."

①

"she went back to the child . . ."

THE SINGER

As she was standing between courtyard and gate,
    she heard
Or thought she heard, a low voice. The child
Called to her, not whining but calling quite sensibly
At least so it seemed to her: "Woman", it said,
    "Help me".
Went on calling not whining but calling quite
    sensibly:
"Don't you know, woman, that she who does not
    listen to a cry for help
But passes by shutting her ears, will never hear
The gentle call of a lover
Nor the blackbird at dawn, nor the happy
Sigh of the exhausted grape-picker at the sound of
the Angelus."
Hearing this
Grusha walks a few steps towards the child and bends
    over it.
she went back to the child
Just for one more look, just to sit with it
For a moment or two till someone should come
Its mother, perhaps, or someone else —
She sits down opposite the child, and leans against a
    trunk.
Just for a moment before she left, for now the
    danger was too great
The city full of flame and grief.

AS GRUSHA

"she went back to the child . . ."

"just for one more look . . ."

RESPONSIVE STORY

"she heard . . ."

"Don't you know, woman,"

". . . will never hear the gentle call of a lover . . ."

②

"Hearing this she went back . . ."

2 Then tell the story once more, using only *responsive* gestures, that is to say, imagine you are emotionally affected by the memory of the incident, the quietness of the first moment, the fascination with the child's tone of voice, the discomfort of indecision before she sits down, the fear of danger, and let your gestures be reactions to those feelings. Give shape, weight and tempo to your gestures. Let them have a beginning, a middle and an end. Be deliberate and make clear choices.

AS THE CHILD, WITH GRUSHA ACTING OUT

The child called to her . . .

3 Now tell the story as though you were the child. Speak to the audience, then to Grusha, and then to the audience as the text requires. Let the child have an attitude to Grusha. It wishes her to protect it. Brecht describes its tone of voice twice. When you have established the child, concentrate on the shift of focus when speaking to the audience and when speaking to Grusha. This change should be clear and sharp. You should make a clear choice as to the exact moment of change. If you have a partner, let your partner play Grusha's part, silently acting out the scene as you tell it.

"'Woman', it said,'Help me'."

③

4 Retell the story as though you were Grusha, remembering the exact moment of her encounter with the child. Imagine that she tells her story in the third person ("As *she* was standing . . .") and in the past, in order to tell it to the audience with absolute accuracy. She tries to remember the exact tone of voice of the child. As she recalls the speech of the child, let her move into the first person present (the here and now) as though hearing the words of the child for the first time. Moving from the past to the present, from the third to the first person, raises the emotional pitch of the story.

". . . till someone should come"

④

"Hearing this . . ."

"she went back to the child . . ."

The following extract from the poem by Bertolt Brecht describes exactly the way a good storyteller moves in and out of character and dramatic action.

Demonstrating his flood of talk she makes it clear . . .

*Young fellows show giggling girls
The way they resist, and in resisting
Slyly flaunt their breasts . . .*

. . . A drunk imitates the preacher . . .

. . . referring the poor to the rich pastures of Paradise . . .

On Everyday Theatre

You artists who perform plays
In great houses under electric suns
Before the hushed crowd, pay a visit some time
To that theatre whose setting is the street.
The everyday, thousandfold, fameless
But vivid, earthy theatre fed by the daily human contact
Which takes place in the street.
Here the woman from next door imitates the landlord:
Demonstrating his flood of talk she makes it clear
How he tried to turn the conversation
From the burst water pipe. In the parks at night
Young fellows show giggling girls
The way they resist, and in resisting
Slyly flaunt their breasts. A drunk
Imitates the preacher at his sermon, referring the poor
To the rich pastures of Paradise. How useful
Such Theatre is though, serious and funny
And how dignified! They do not, like parrot or ape
Imitate just for the sake of imitation, unconcerned
What they imitate, just to show that they
Can imitate; no, they
Have a point to put across. You
Great artists, masterly imitators, in this regard
Do not fall short of them! Do not become too remote

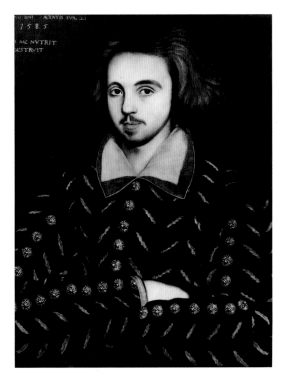

Marlowe changed the course of English drama.

Christopher Marlowe (1564-93)

Christopher Marlowe, English playwright and poet, was also an alleged spy, atheist, blasphemous subversive and homosexual. He was knifed to death in a pub in Deptford at the age of 29. He is credited with many of the dramatic innovations which were to flower into Elizabethan drama, combining the physical vigor of the old religious medieval theatre with the technical elegance and sophisticated imagery of Renaissance poetry. In particular, he developed the use of the iambic pentameter. This was used for the famous free verse of speech and became the medium of communication for all Elizabethan playwrights, including Shakespeare.

His plays are epic in all respects, and *Tamburlaine the Great* (1587) established Marlowe's reputation. It employs a wide time-span, many locations, combines comedy and tragedy, and is episodic in structure.

Marlowe specialized in the creation of roles for men of overweening ambition. *The Massacre at Paris* (1589), *The Jew of Malta* (1589) and *The Tragical History of Dr Faustus* (c. 1592) are all driven by an ambitious hero. The roles were played by the powerful and bombastic Edward Alleyn, who made his fortune creating Marlowe's epic roles.

Tamburlaine, one of Marlowe's bombastic heroes.

A romantic nineteenth-century view of Marlowe's death.

Chapter 8

Realism

Theatre of Observed Reality

The idea that ordinary people can have dramatic lives is relatively new. The social observation of nineteenth-century novelists, combined with a growing interest in the psychological lives of characters, paved the way for this new style of theatre.

It may seem odd to us that the creation of play texts through the observation of everyday life is a fairly recent phenomenon. The process began in the 1730s, with the invention of domestic tragedy. Playwrights felt for the first time that it might be possible to find drama in the lives of people who were not kings, queens or demi-gods. Konrad Ekhof (1720–78), the favorite actor of Gotthold Lessing (1729–81), the German dramatist and drama critic, worked hard to transform acting to fit the new writing. Ekhof suggested that two qualities were required in the actor in order to properly play these new roles. These were empathy (the ability to assume the emotional attitude your character takes towards the world) and observation (the ability to recreate observed behavior). These two talents are essential to the work of the modern realistic actor.

The main impetus for realism came from the French naturalistic novelists in the latter half of the nineteenth century, notably from Emile Zola (1840–1902), whose dramatization of his novel *Thérèse Raquin* is regarded as the first realistic drama. Realism represents unheroic everyday contemporary life. Its settings are related to what can be observed in the real world, as are the characters, who have consistency and coherence. The problems the plays tackle are modern, voiced in terms that would credibly fit the speech of ordinary people of our own time.

The difference between naturalism and realism is of production values rather than style. A naturalistic production would include every possible element of observable reality in terms of props, setting and costume. In fact, realistic writers like the Norwegian Henrik Ibsen (1828–1906), the Russian Anton Chekhov (1860–1904) and the American Arthur Miller

(1915–) frequently mix expressionist and symbolist episodes into their realistic plays.

Zola liked the term "real" in realism, but realism is a *style*, rather than reality itself. Time, for example, is almost always compressed. Realistic drama does not take place in real time. The coincidence of events, chance meetings, misfortunes, fallings in love, dramatic encounters far surpass the probability of reality. The purpose of a realistic world is to *seem* natural. This is why Ibsen regarded the scenario (the detailed draft of the plot) as the center of his craft. Ibsen would often take more time to construct a seamless plot, making its artificial coincidences appear natural, than he would to write the play.

Realism uses the elements and signs of observed reality as its language, but another psychological language lies below the surface. Konstantin Stanislavsky (1863–1938) and Vladimir Nemirovich-Danchenko (1858–1943) founded the Moscow Art Theatre in 1898, only two years before Sigmund Freud (1856–1939) published *The Interpretation of Dreams*. Stanislavsky began to invent exercises in psychological observation which were particularly appropriate to Chekhov's plays. In this world the characters present stable public personalities often in contrast to their shattered inner lives. Stanislavsky began to explore the dynamic inner lives of Chekhov's characters. The drama of the common man had come of age.

Chekhov wished the audience to feel as though they were eavesdropping on very private conversations. This sort of realism demands intense attention from an audience, while creating an intimacy within which the audience can become deeply involved with the characters.

145

Henrik Ibsen (1828-1906)

Ibsen, social critic and exposer of society's secrets.

The Norwegian playwright Henrik Ibsen began his career as stage director at the new Norwegian Theatre in Bergen. After a succession of struggles with the practical business of theatre, Ibsen left Norway for Rome in 1864 – the start of a 27-year self-imposed exile.

Ibsen then produced large-scale poetic dramas, such as *Brand* (1865) and *Peer Gynt* (1867), and next began to move towards dramas of social realism. He abandoned verse for what he called the "more difficult medium of everyday speech," and started to create psychological drama with complex, realistic characterization in the setting of the comfortable middle-class drawing room. These plays explore the struggle for individual freedom in a suffocating social environment. Such subtleties were not appreciated by Ibsen's contemporaries, who saw no further than the subject matter. *A Doll's House* (1879) dealt with a young wife who walks out on her family and was seen as a shocking feminist tract. *Ghosts* (1881) used the theme of inherited syphilis to expose social illness and disease. The *Daily Telegraph* critic, Clement Scott, called it "an open drain, a loathesome sore." Like all world-class realistic drama, observable realism resonates beyond itself, in Ibsen's case by exploring forbidden social themes through relationships.

A scene from Ghosts, *which dramatized a shocking illness.*

Ibsen was to continue to develop psychological realism away from the social struggle and towards the inner struggles of his characters. In such plays as *The Lady from the Sea* (1888), *Hedda Gabler* (1891) and *The Master Builder* (1892), the inner claims of ideal vision and practical compromise engage in mortal combat. His influence upon twentieth-century drama is colossal. In spite of the violent controversy surrounding his plays, he was able to establish the theatre as a means of serious debate.

Hedda Gabler, one of Ibsen's extraordinary female characters.

Anton Chekhov (1860-1904)

Chekhov was a doctor by training, whose writing began in an effort to support his vast, impoverished family. He was a successful writer of short stories, which were heavily influenced by Russian realist writers such as Leo Tolstoy (1828–1910) and Ivan Turgenev (1818–83). His own subtle and compassionate powers of observation led him to link apparently eccentric details in the behavior of his characters into significant patterns, and to allow the dramatic, comic and tragic aspects of their lives to be revealed through the apparent trivia of their everyday existence.

Chekhov, the master of compassionate observation.

Chekhov's early one-act plays, such as *The Bear* (1888) and *The Proposal* (1890), are examples of farces based on his short stories. *On the High Road* (1884) and *Swan Song* (1888) are tear-jerking melodramas. These early plays offer very conventional, derivative material, but Chekhov used them to master stage technique after the failure of his early, long plays.

Chekhov's major plays, *The Seagull* (1896), *Uncle Vanya* (1899), *Three Sisters* (1901) and *The Cherry Orchard* (1904) suffered initially because the actors played in a broad-farce acting style wholly inappropriate to the world of the play. They were all staged by Stanislavsky at the Moscow Art Theatre in what for Chekhov were unsatisfactory, sentimental and naturalistic productions. Nevertheless, these productions were to make Chekhov the most celebrated early twentieth-century Russian dramatist known to the West. His plays are remarkable to us for their psychological realism. By strictly controlling the expression of overt dramatic action, Chekhov focuses upon the yearning inner lives of his characters. Time marches on inexorably as they fritter away the potential of their lives in an endless trail of triviality. Apparently devoid of action, the action in fact lies in the psychological inner worlds of the characters, which appear to us in turn amusing and tragic. In his plays, Chekhov brought observed realism to a new depth and sophistication.

A scene from Three Sisters.

The seagull resonates as both a living thing and an image.

Unselfconscious acting, in which the audience eavesdrops on the conversation.

The Cherry Orchard by Anton Chekhov

CONCEALED SUBTEXT

"Say it. Say it."

This exercise is aimed at helping you to explore the use of subtext.

In Greek tragedy or Shakespeare, characters usually say what they mean. If they are lying, they will usually find a way to tell you – the audience – what they're doing. In life we often cannot say what we mean. Sometimes this is because of the rules of the society in which the play is set. For example, men and women who were not on socially acceptable intimate terms would, before the 1950s, have had to be very careful how they expressed their feelings for each other. This is part of the world of the play. Personality or character obviously also plays a part since few people are able to be frank and direct about their feelings without shocking or causing offence to others. Chekhov was a great observer of this human trait. His characters often use words to hide their feelings rather than to express them. In other words, there is "subtext" in the scene: this is what they would really like to say rather than what they actually say.

"Be kind. Wait for the right moment."

"What am I pretending to look for?"

Exercise

The Hidden Text

This is a scene from the last act of *The Cherry Orchard*. Lopakhin, a rich man descended from serfs, has achieved his life's ambition and bought the "Cherry Orchard." The old landowners must move out and are catching the train. Lopakhin is persuaded to see Varia, an adopted daughter of the old owners, before she leaves with the family. Everybody in the household has always assumed that these two would marry, and this is Lopakhin's last chance to propose. In this dialogue, I have suggested a subtext for the first few lines. The dots in the text are Chekhov's way of indicating that the character has inhibited his or her own thought process. Speak the line and speak the hidden subtext (what the character wanted but was unable to say, or how the character would have continued the line beyond the dots, if he or she had the courage). Inventing subtext will make you specifically aware of how your character is actually communicating. My subtext is written in bold and is in square brackets.

Varia and Lopakhin. Varia is packing her clothes for her departure.

EXPRESSING SUBTEXT

"The moment is passing away, say something."

"Wait for the right moment."

"The moment is passing away . . ."

". . . say something."

(Suppressed whispering and laughter is heard from behind the door, and finally VARIA comes in [I'm suffocating. I'll die. Everyone is laughing at me. I can't look him in the eye.] *and starts examining the luggage. After some time she says:)* [This is unbearable.]

VARIA
It's strange, I just can't find . . . [Oh God, what am I pretending to look for?]

LOPAKHIN
[How do you do this? Be kind.] What are you looking for? [Wait for the right moment.]

VARIA
[Say it. Say it.] I packed the things myself, yet I can't remember . . . . [The moment is passing away, say something.] *A pause.*

LOPAKHIN
[I mustn't rush things. I mustn't frighten her.] Where are you going now, Varvara Mihailovna? [This is a polite way to say "Varia"]

VARIA
[Away forever.] I? To the Rogulins. I've agreed to look after the house for them . . . to be their housekeeper, or something.

LOPAKHIN
That's at Yashnevo, isn't it? About seventy miles from here. *(A pause.)* So this is the end of life in this house . . .

VARIA
(Examining the luggage) But where could it be? Or perhaps I've packed it in the trunk? . . . Yes, life in this house has come to an end . . . there won't be any more . . .

LOPAKHIN
I'm going to Kharkov presently . . . . On the next train . . . . I've got a lot to do there . . . . And I'm leaving Yepihodov here . . . . I've engaged him.

VARIA
Well! . . .

LOPAKHIN
Do you remember, last year about this time it was snowing already, but now it's quite still and sunny. It's rather cold, though . . . . About three degrees of frost.

VARIA
I haven't looked . . . *(A pause.)* Besides, our thermometer's broken . . . . *(A pause.)*
A voice calls Lopakhin

LOPAKHIN
(As though he had been expecting it.) Coming this moment! *(He leaves quickly.)*
Varia, sitting on the floor with her head in a bundle of clothes, sobs softly.

The following exercise can be used for any psychologically realistic play. It allows you to test how constrained your character is by the rules of the world of the play, and by your character's personality traits.

Lopakhin expresses his feelings for Varia.

Talking within the conventions of the world of the play.

Exercise

Finding the Subtext in the World of the Play

You should be at a stage where you are sure of your character, and you should work with a partner. You are going to explore the relationship between your character and the character your partner is playing. Use Lopakhin and Varia if you wish. You should know about the world of the play, and what constitutes "good manners." Both of you should go "into character" and sit opposite each other.

One character will talk, and the other will listen. First, say everything you can about your relationship to the character opposite you. *You must not stray from the social conventions of the play.* Your speech, behavior, manners and the subjects you broach must be acceptable to the conventions of the world of the play. Now say

everything you feel, but cannot say because of the world contained within the play.

How much extra material is released in the second part of the exercise? What effect does it have on the character? Discuss how accurate you were and how true to the world of the play.

Next, you should swap roles. The partner who talked now listens. Make the rules of behavior more specific as you work.

Varia expresses her feelings for Lopakhin without regard for conventions.

Psychological Orientation

WHO AM I?

The character's
background? Education?
Family? Relationships?
Social influences? Taste, e.g. in clothes?
Physical and emotional make-up, characteristics?

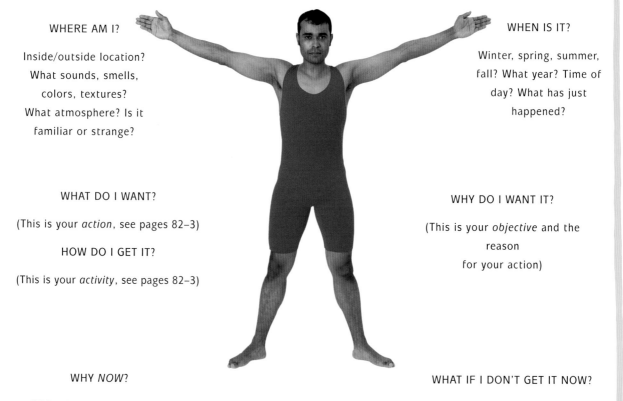

WHERE AM I?

Inside/outside location?
What sounds, smells,
colors, textures?
What atmosphere? Is it
familiar or strange?

WHEN IS IT?

Winter, spring, summer,
fall? What year? Time of
day? What has just
happened?

WHAT DO I WANT?

(This is your *action*, see pages 82–3)

HOW DO I GET IT?

(This is your *activity*, see pages 82–3)

WHY DO I WANT IT?

(This is your *objective* and the
reason
for your action)

WHY *NOW*?

(This gives you *immediacy*)

WHAT IF I DON'T GET IT NOW?

(This gives you the *stakes* – the
consequences of failure)

WHAT MUST I OVERCOME?

(This is the *obstacle* or
resistance and is your
problem in the scene)

Konstantin Stanislavsky (1863–1938)

Konstantin Stanislavsky was a Russian actor, producer and teacher.

It will be said, "But what kind of truth can this be, when all on the stage is a lie, an imitation, scenery, cardboard, paint, make up, properties, wooden goblets, swords and spears? Is this all truth?" But it is not of this truth I speak. I speak of the truth of emotions, of the truth of inner creative urges which strain forward to find expression, of the truth of the memories of bodily and physical perceptions. I am not interested in a truth that is without myself; I am interested in the truth that is within myself . . .

Konstantin Stanislavsky, *My Life in Art*, 1924

Stanislavsky, the creator and teacher of methodical preparation.

Eugene Vakhtangov (1833–1922)

Eugene Vakhtangov was Konstantin Stanislavsky's greatest pupil and disciple.

Critics of Stanislavskii's doctrine often overlook the statement which takes first place in the system and methods of Stanislavskii: that the actor should not be concerned about his feelings during the play, it will come of itself. They label as auto-suggestion and narcotic self intoxication the help which Stanislavskii gives to students in recalling their intimate experiences. But Stanislavskii maintained the opposite: don't try to experience, don't make feelings to order, forget about them altogether. In life our feelings come to us by themselves against our will. Our willing gives birth to action directed towards the gratification of desire. If we succeed in gratifying it, a positive feeling is born spontaneously. If an obstacle stands in the way of gratifying it, a negative feeling is born – "suffering".

From the diary of Eugene Vakhtangov

Eleonora Duse
(1858-1924)

Eleonora Duse was the leading Italian actress of the
late nineteenth century, and was a great inspiration to
Konstantin Stanislavsky. George Bernard Shaw,
commenting on her acting in *Our Theatres in the Nineties*,
said: "I should say without qualification that it is the
best modern acting I have ever seen . . . behind every
stroke of it is a distinctively human idea." Chekhov
may have had her in mind when he wrote *The Seagull*,
and she was admired for her roles in Ibsen's plays,
including the part of Hedda Gabler.

*Arthur Miller's plays have, famously, dissected the
issues of American social and political life.*

*Eleonora Duse
brought restraint
and serious
purpose to the
grand tradition of
romantic realism.*

*Act? What a nasty word! If acting were all there was to it; I
feel that I have never known nor shall I ever know how to
act! Those poor women in my plays have entered so totally
into my heart and head, that while I am striving as best I can
to make the audience understand them, I almost feel like
comforting them . . . but it is they who, little by little, succeed
in comforting me!*

Letter to D'Archais, 1885

Arthur Miller (1915-   )

Arthur Miller is America's greatest living playwright. He is included here as a realist playwright although, like Chekhov and Ibsen, he mixes symbolist and expressionist episodes into his realistic texts. He explores the tragedy of ordinary people, and his many essays on modern tragedy (*The Theater Essays of Arthur Miller*, 1971) oppose the contention of George Steiner that tragedy cannot exist in the modern age. Miller's early work is sometimes labelled "New Realism," and is heavily influenced by Ibsen.

In Miller's plays, relationships resonate beyond themselves and comment on social issues.

After the failure of *The Man Who Had All The Luck* (1944), Miller rapidly rose to fame with *All My Sons* (1947) and *Death of a Salesman* (1947). In these plays he displayed his great ability to address burning issues of contemporary American social and political life through the domestic lives of his characters. *The Crucible* (1953) drew parallels between the seventeenth-century Salem witch trials and the McCarthy witch-hunts – at fever pitch at the time he wrote the play. *A View from the Bridge* (1955) is a tragedy set in an immigrant community. Miller was married to Marilyn Monroe from 1955 to 1961, returning to the stage in 1964 with *After the Fall* (1963), *Incident at Vichy* and *The Price* (1968).

A scene from The Crucible, *Miller's ruthless dissection of witch-hunts.*

His latest play, *Broken Glass* (1994), is set in Brooklyn in late November, 1938. The American community, which is "in deep spiritual disorganization," is unable properly to respond to German racism. Sylvia Gellburg, physically absorbing the news of the atrocity of *Kristallnacht* – the night during which Germans rose up as a people and attacked Jews – loses the use of her legs. Miller says that his play is concerned with "a public concern and a private neurosis." The problem is "to find that juncture where they actually meet." This is the purpose of all Miller's major plays.

Glossary

Ad lib To improvise a speech, especially when someone has forgotten their lines.

Apron The part of the stage that extends beyond the curtain toward the audience. It is sometimes called the forestage.

Auditorium The area of the theatre where the audience sits.

Backdrop The drape or painted canvas that masks the back of the stage.

Backstage The areas that surround the stage, including the dressing rooms.

Blackout The term used for when the stage is suddenly plunged into darkness.

Book, the The actor's text. To be "off the book" means that you have learned your lines.

Box set This is a hard surround made up of three walls, including "real" doors and sometimes a ceiling. It represents an interior setting.

Business This is the term used for the physical activities of an actor, which reveal his or her character during a performance.

Crew The people (other than actors) who build and operate the production.

Cue Any pre-arranged signal (a word, a light or some business) that tells the actor or stage manager to proceed with the action.

Curtain call The term used for when the cast walk on-stage to bow.

Downstage (Toward) the front of the stage.

Ensemble Playing together as a company, rather than as "stars" and "extras."

Entrance, an The effectiveness with which an actor walks on to the stage.

Epilogue A speech spoken by an actor directly to the audience after the conclusion of a play.

Fit-up, the The term used for when the set and lights are put in place.

Flat A piece of scenery made from canvas stretched over a wooden frame.

Flies The space above the stage into which scenery can be hoisted.

Flood A stage light without a lens that "washes" light on to the stage.

Footlights A row of lights along the front of the stage.

Front of house This is the area where the audience gather before a show or during the intermission.

Get in/out To construct or dismantle and remove the set.

Grid The frame above the auditorium/stage on which the lights are hung.

Mark out, to To mark a plan of the stage area on the rehearsal room floor.

Mask, to To cut off the view of the audience, perhaps using flats. An actor may also mask another actor.

Off-stage In the wings or backstage.

On-stage In view of the audience.

Pace The rhythm of playing a scene.

Prologue A speech by a player, spoken to the audience before the play begins.

Prompt To remind an actor of his or her lines during a performance.

Prompt copy A script that is marked with all light/sound cues and the actors' moves.

Proscenium This is the frame that surrounds the front, or opening, of a traditional stage.

Rake, the The slope sometimes found on a stage, which goes upward toward the back of the stage.

Set All the scenery of a production.

Strike, to To dismantle and remove the set.

Upstage Away from the audience.

Walk down, the See **Curtain call**.

Wings The space to the left and right of the stage.

Working lights The lights that are used by the technical crew.

Index

Further Reading

If you enjoy books about the nature and meaning of theatre, the role of theatre in society and the role of the actor, you should read the following:

Barker, H., *Arguments for a Theatre,* Manchester University Press
Brook, P., *There are no Secrets,* Methuen
Brook, P., *The Empty Space,* Penguin
Miller & Martin, *The Theatre Essays of Arthur Miller,* Methuen

If you are interested in Stanislavskii's contribution to the theory and practice of modern acting, try:

Gordon, M., *The Stanislavskii Technique – Russia,* Applause
Hagen, U., & Frankle, H., *Respect for Acting,* Macmillan

The following books combine history and theory with many practical exercises:

Johnstone, K., *Impro,* Methuen
Suzuki, T., *The Way of Acting,* Theatre Communications Ltd

For a strongly psychological-physical approach to text interpretation and character transformation read:

Checkov, M., *On the Technique of Acting,* Harper Collins
Hodgson, J., *Mastering Movement – Understanding Laban,* Methuen

Finally, for vocal and text work, try:

Berry, C., *The Actor and his Text,* Harrap
McCallion, M., *The Voice Book,* Faber

Acknowledgments

Key **a** above, **b** below,
c center, **l** left, **r** right

Ace Photo Agency **88ar**
(A & J Verkaik), **89c** (Roger
Howard), **89r** (Colin Thomas);
Catherine Ashmore **147c**;
Barnaby's Picture Library
(Gerald Clyde) **125a**; Dahlstrom
Photography/
Portland Center for the
Performing Arts **72**; Dominic
Photography (Richard H. Smith)
143bl, **155a**; Zoe Dominic
146bl, **147bc**, & **br**; Hulton
Getty Picture Collection **113**,
143al, **146al**, **154ar**; Robbie
Jack **2**, **5ar**, **107ar**, **br** & **al**,
114br, **115cl**, **119l**, **125b**,
129a, **135**, **146c**, **148bl**, **155b**,
Mander & Mitchenson **138ar** &
br, **139l** & **r**, **153**; Mansell
Collection **115ar**, **143br**,
147ar, **154**; New Victoria
Theatre, Stoke-on-Trent,
Staffordshire **73**; Anthony
O'Driscoll **119r**; Orange Tree
Theatre, Richmond, Surrey **74**;
Panic Picture Library (Chris
Pearce) **4ar**, **5br**, **115br**, **123r**,
128, **129b**; Pictor International
104; Tara Arts Company (Dave

Corio) **136**; John Vickers
Theatre Collection **4**, **114al**.

All other photographs are the
copyright of Quarto Publishing
plc.

Quarto would like to
acknowledge and thank Dancia
International. Drury Lane,
London WC2, who kindly loaned
shoes used in photography.

Dorothy Frame for the index.

Text acknowledgments

The Miser in *The Miser and Other
Plays* by Moliére, translated by
John Wood (Penquin Classics,
1953) copyright (c) John Wood,
1953. Reproduced by permission
of Penquin Books Ltd.
The Cherry Orchard in *Plays by
Anton Chekov*, translated by
Elisaveta Fen (Penquin Classics,
1951) copyright (c) Elisaveta
Fen, 1951. Reproduced by
permission of Penquin Books
Ltd.
'On Everyday Theatre' by
Bertolt Brecht in *Bertolt Brecht,
Poems 1913-1956*, edited by John

Willet & Ralph Manheim with
the cooperation of Erich Fried,
Eyre Methuen Ltd 1976.
Reproduced by permission of
Reed Books and Routledge Inc.
The Caucasian Chalk Circle by
Bertolt Brecht in *Brecht Plays 3*,
translated by Stern/Auden,
Methuen Drama 1987.
Reproduced by permission of
Reed Books and Routledge Inc.
Spring Awakening by Frank
Wedekind, translated by Edward
Bond, Methuen. Reproduced by
permission of Reed Books.
*The Theatre Essays of Arthur
Mille*r, edited by Robert A.
Martin. Reproduced by
permission of Reed Books.
Actors on Acting by Toby and
Helen Chinoy, Crown Publishing
Group.

The publishers have made every
effort to contact copyright
holders where they can be found.
The publishers will be happy to
include any missing copyright
acknowledgments in future
editions.

Quarto would especially like to thank the models:

Chloë Mostyn   Christian (Tim) Greger   Marianne Larsen   Gary Calandro